Doodle-Dos:

Zentangles

Other Available Coloring Book Titles—

Doodle-dos: Celebration of Glorious Crowns—
"Life's too short for boring hair!"

Doodle-dos: Whimsical Waves

ISBN: 978-0-9982339-9-4

Manufactured in the U.S.A.

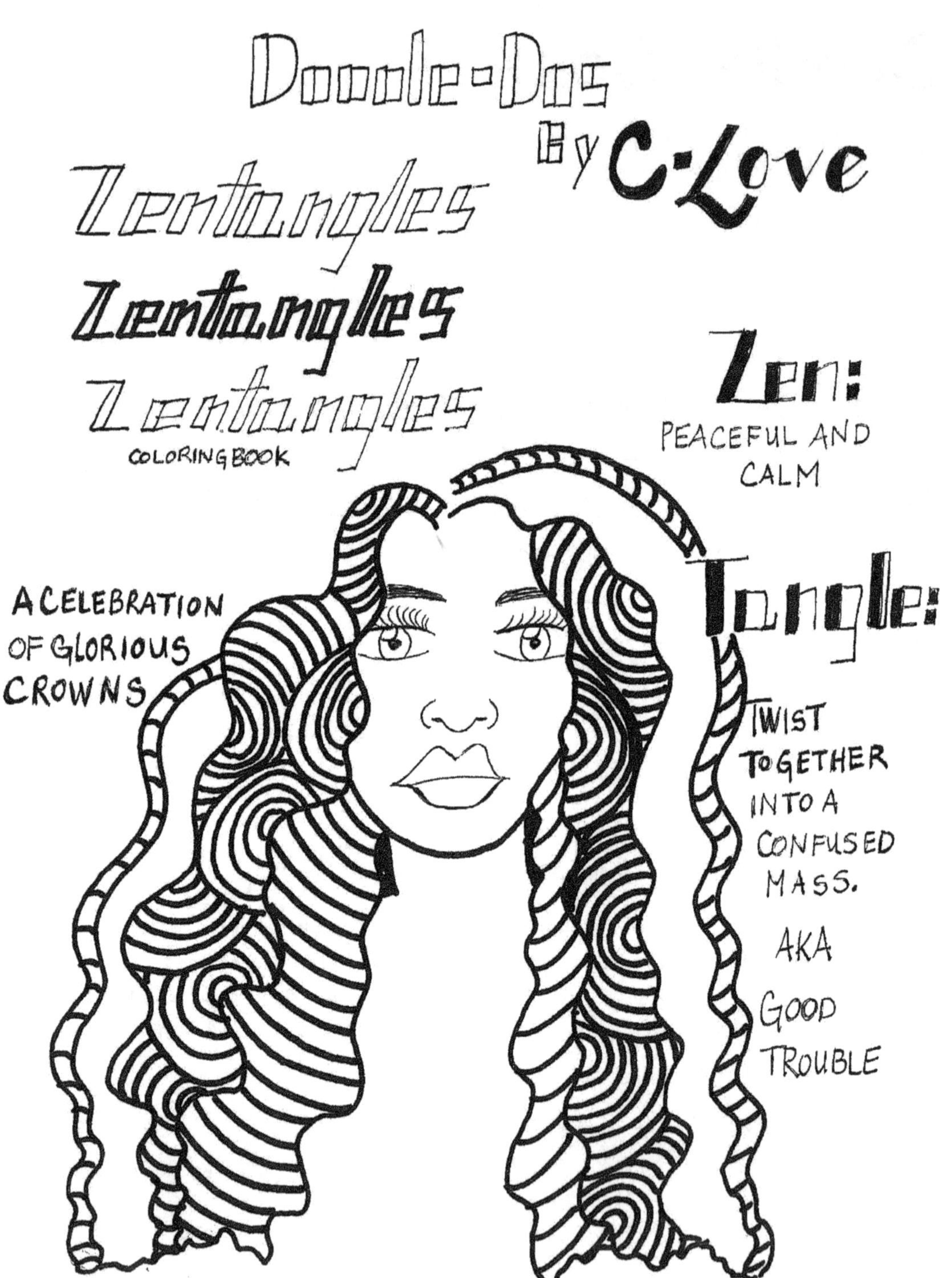
Doodle-Dos
By C-Love
Zentangles
Zentangles
Zentangles
COLORING BOOK
Zen:
PEACEFUL AND CALM
A CELEBRATION OF GLORIOUS CROWNS
Tangle:
TWIST TOGETHER INTO A CONFUSED MASS.
AKA
GOOD TROUBLE

Doodle-Dos

"Zentangles" comes from the studio of C-Love.

This fun, detailed coloring book is full of inspired designs and surprises.

Doodle-Do = "Hair-do" made of shapes, lines, numbers, squiggles, zigzags, and swirls.

GRAB YOUR PENCIL, PEN, MARKERS, AND/OR CRAYONS – Let's go half on a masterpiece.

"Instead of focusing on what you can control, Focus on what you can create."

FREE STUFF?

COLOR POST TAG
@welovedoodledos (IG)
Come get yourself some freebies.

THANKYOU FOR PURCHASING THIS COLORING BOOK. PLEASE RELAX, CLEAR YOUR MIND AND COLOR AWAY. FOR THOSE WHO ENJOY DOODLING AS MUCH AS I DO — I HOPE YOU ENJOY THE SURPRISES!

ENJOY,

C-Love

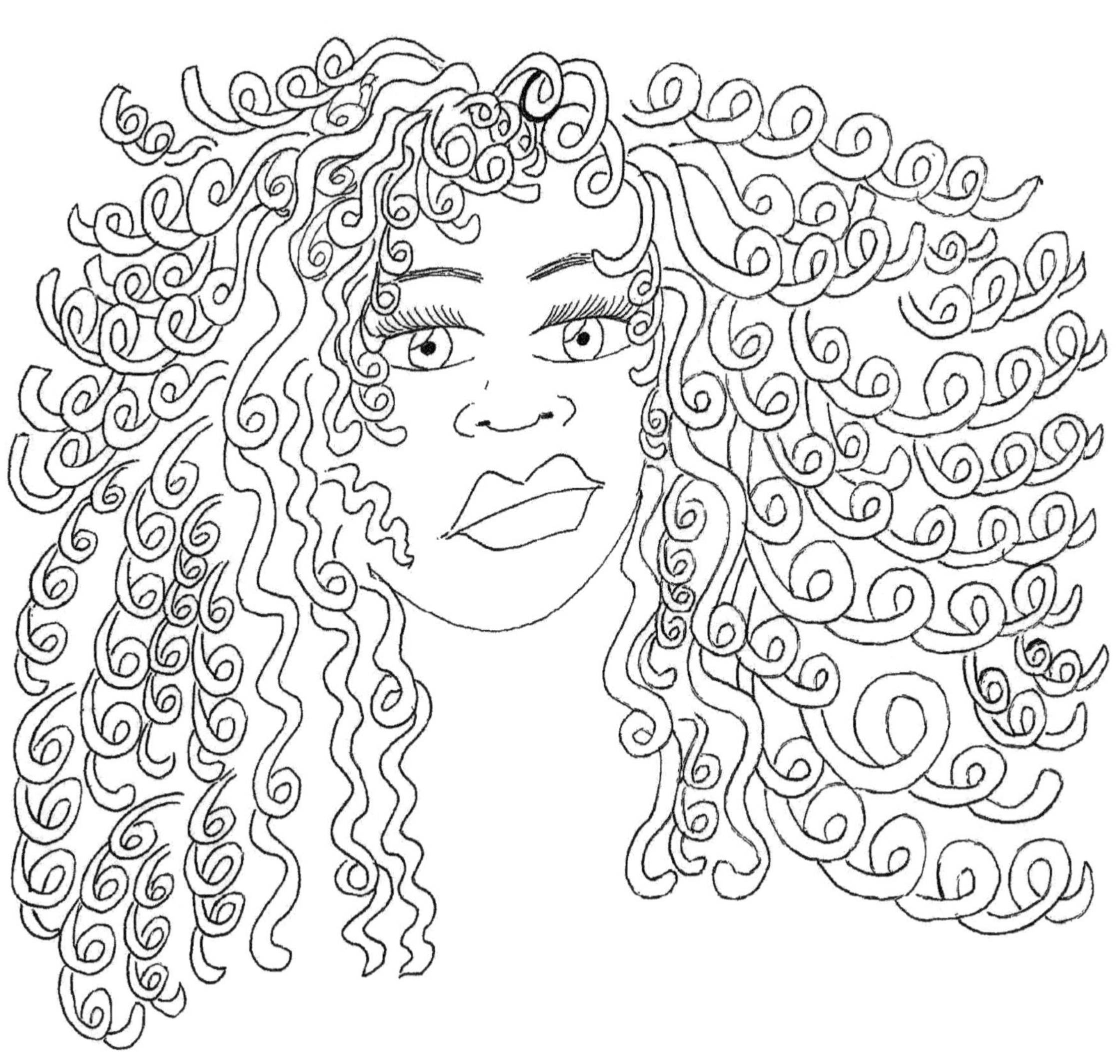

My Truth Matters

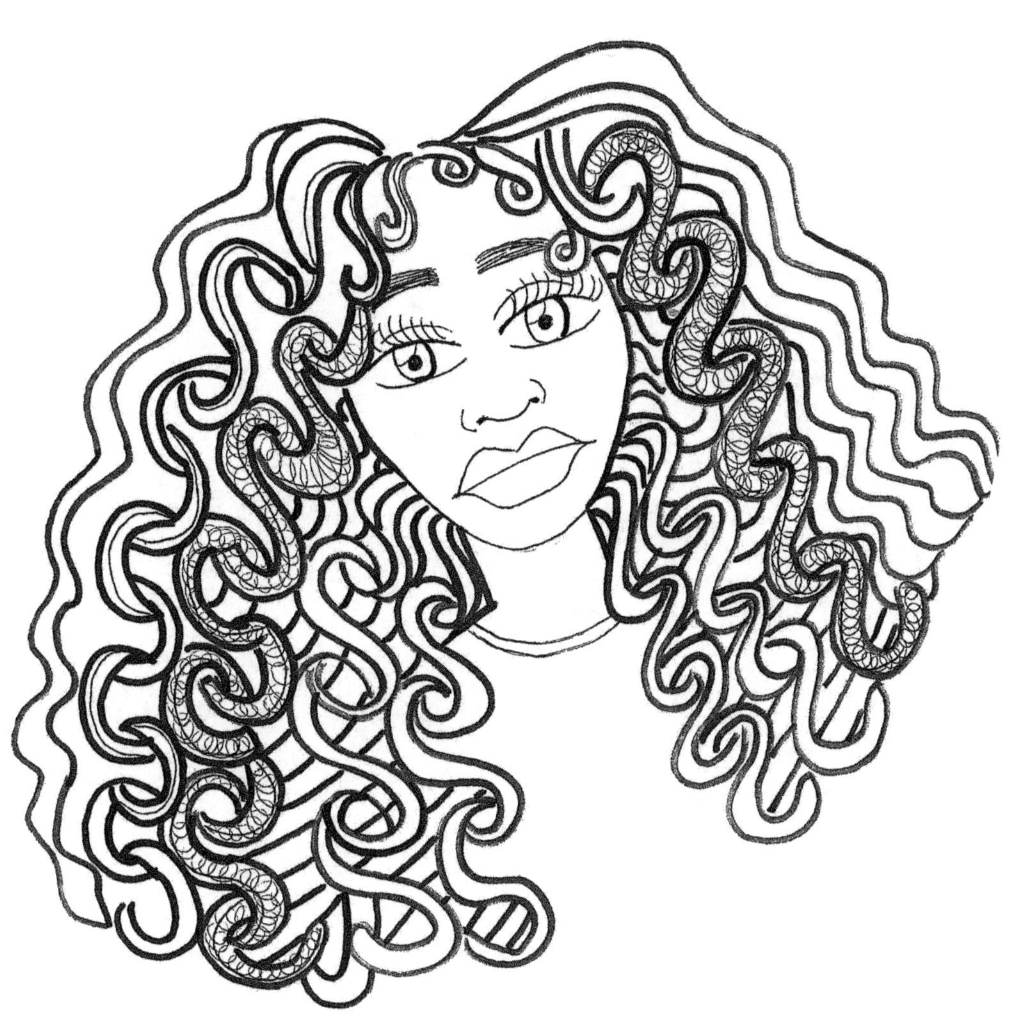

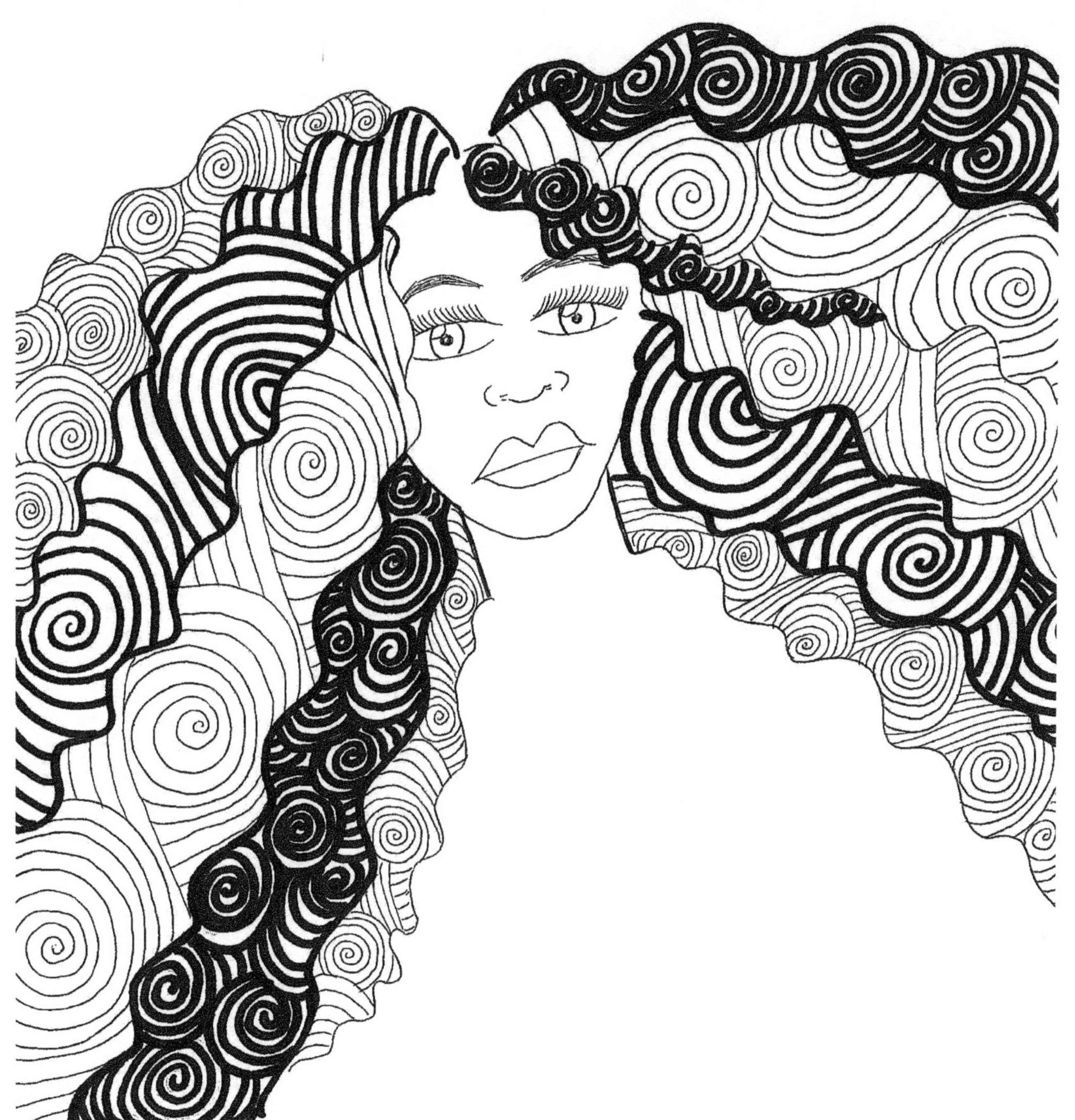

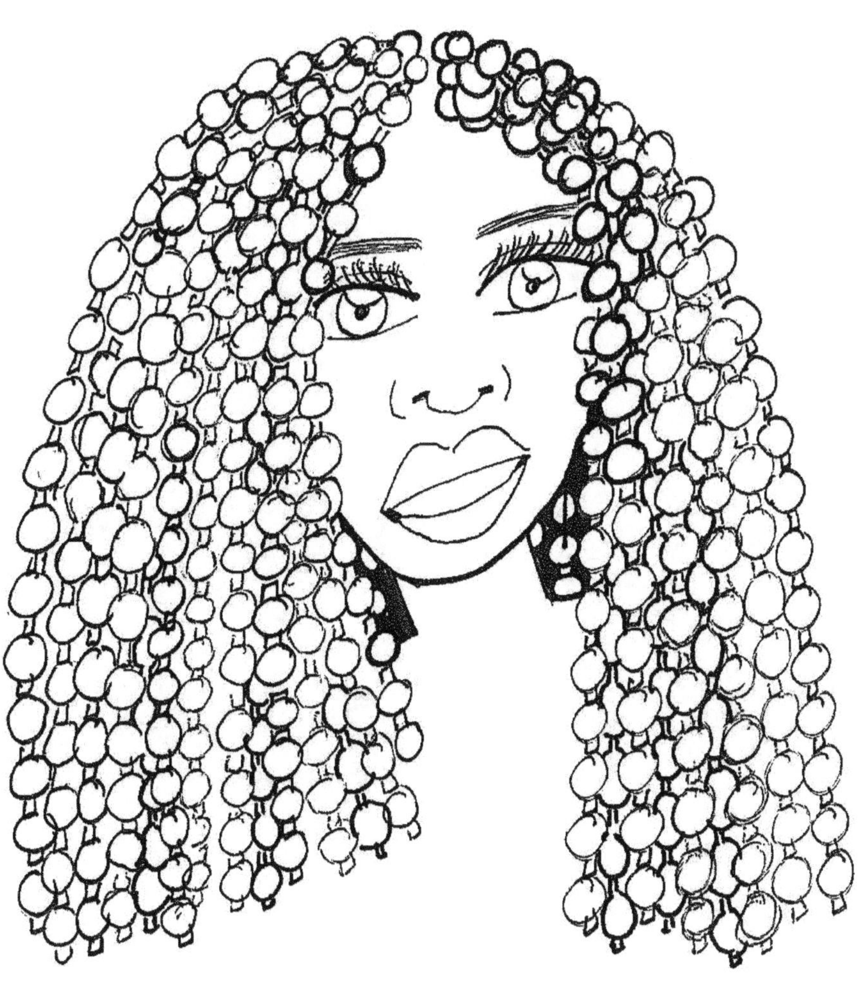

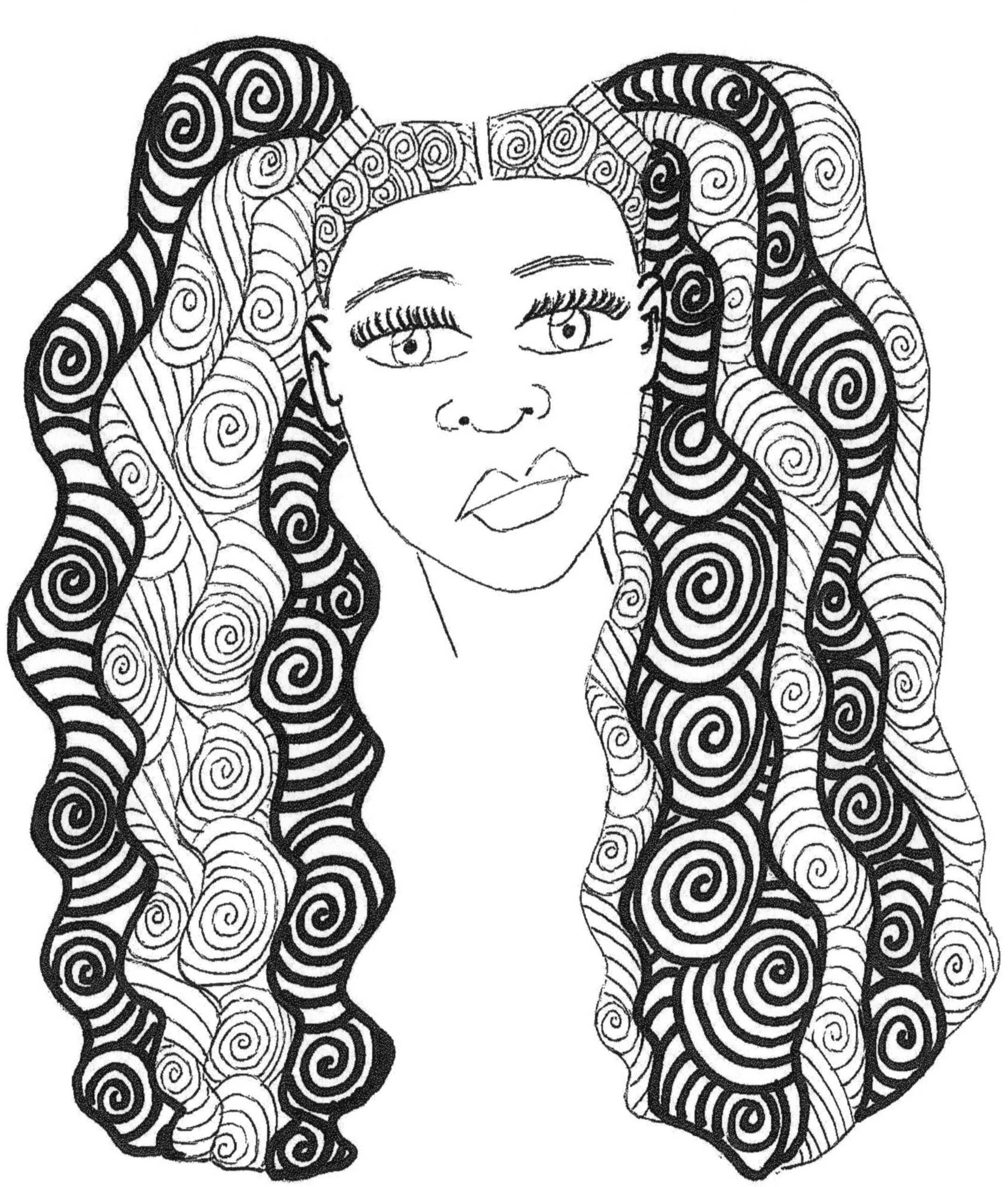

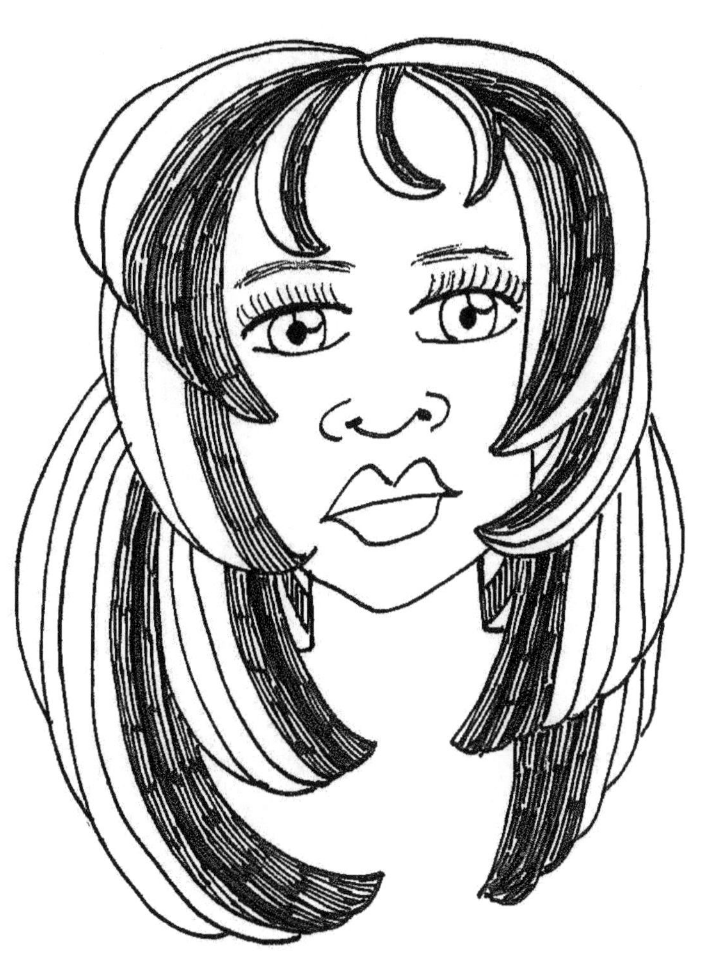

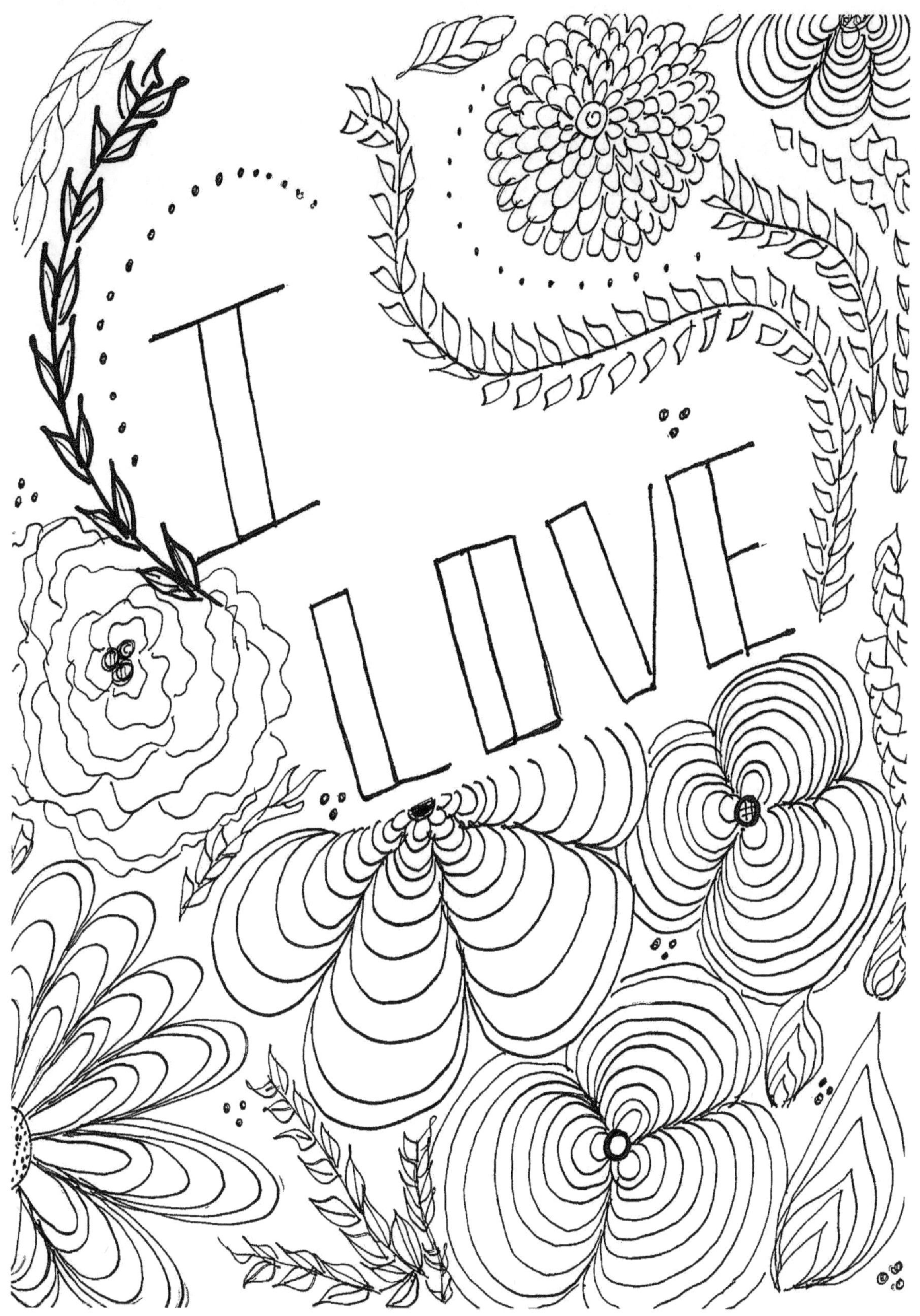
I
LIVE

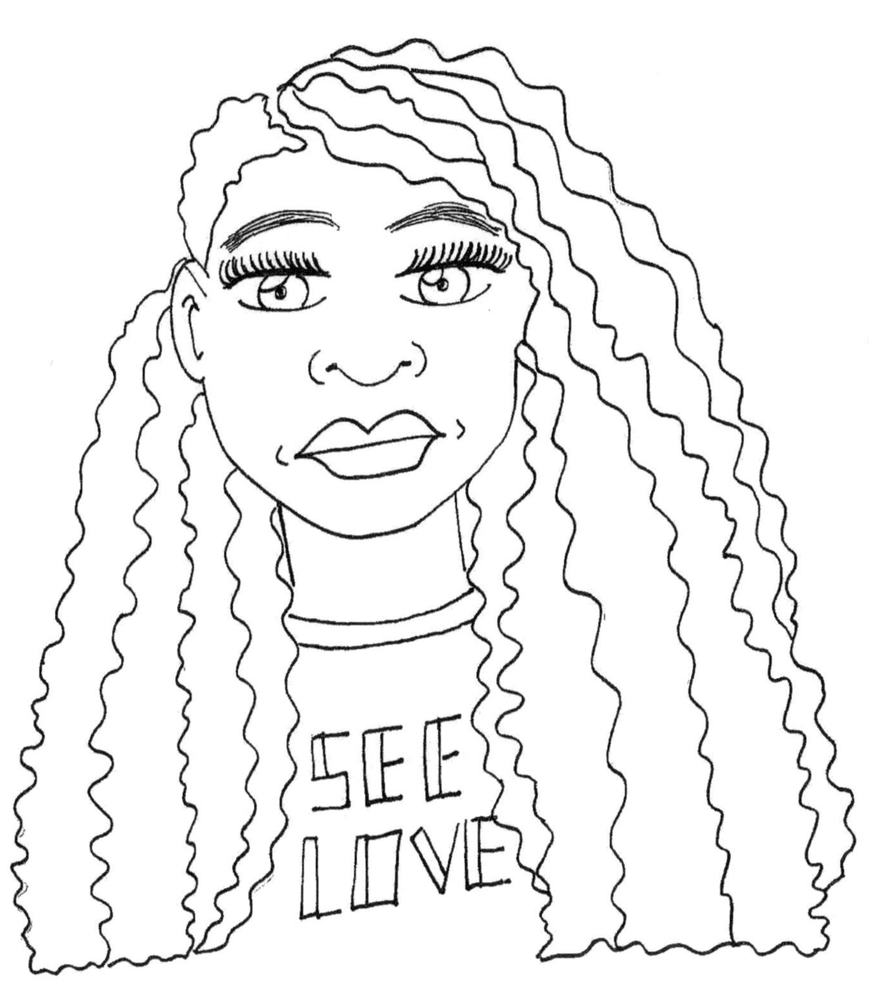
SEE
LOVE

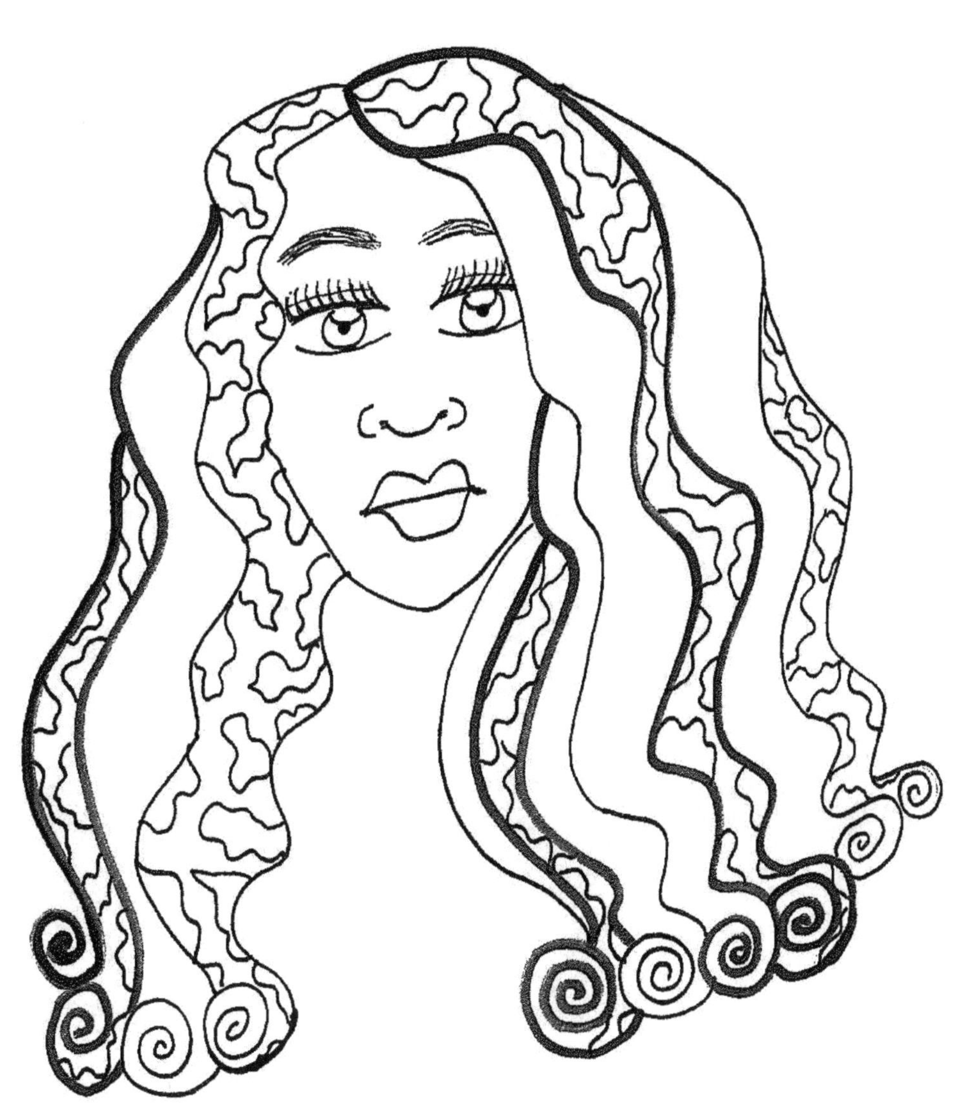

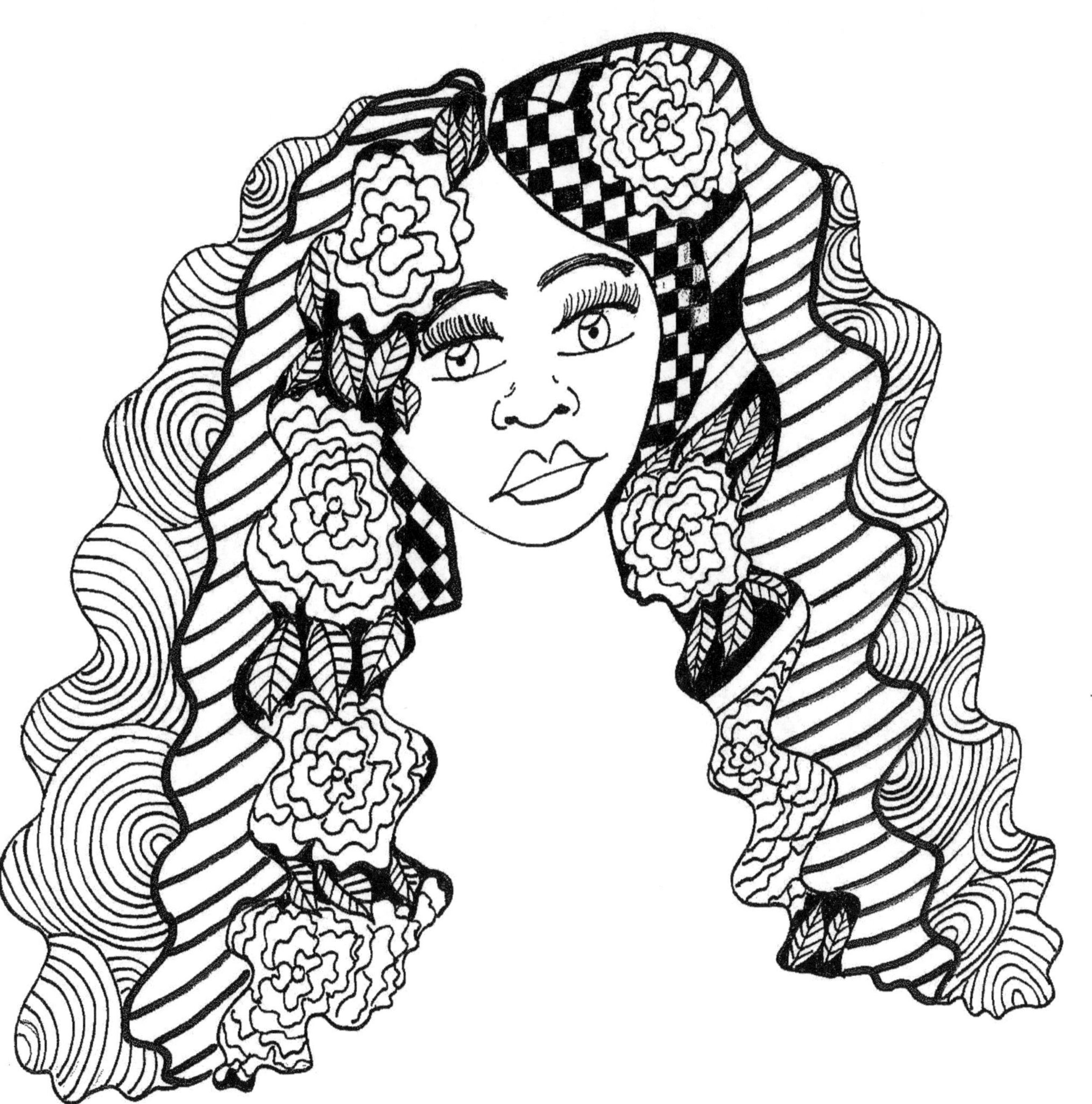

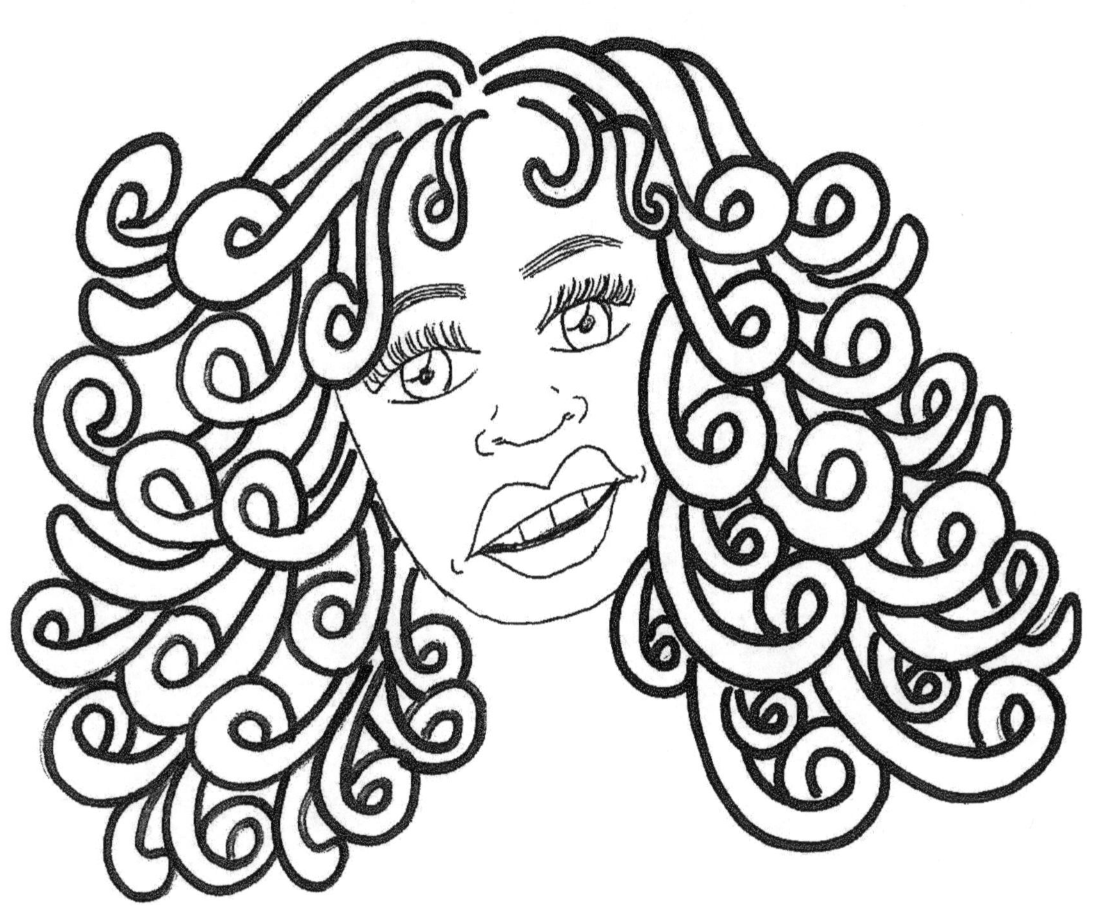

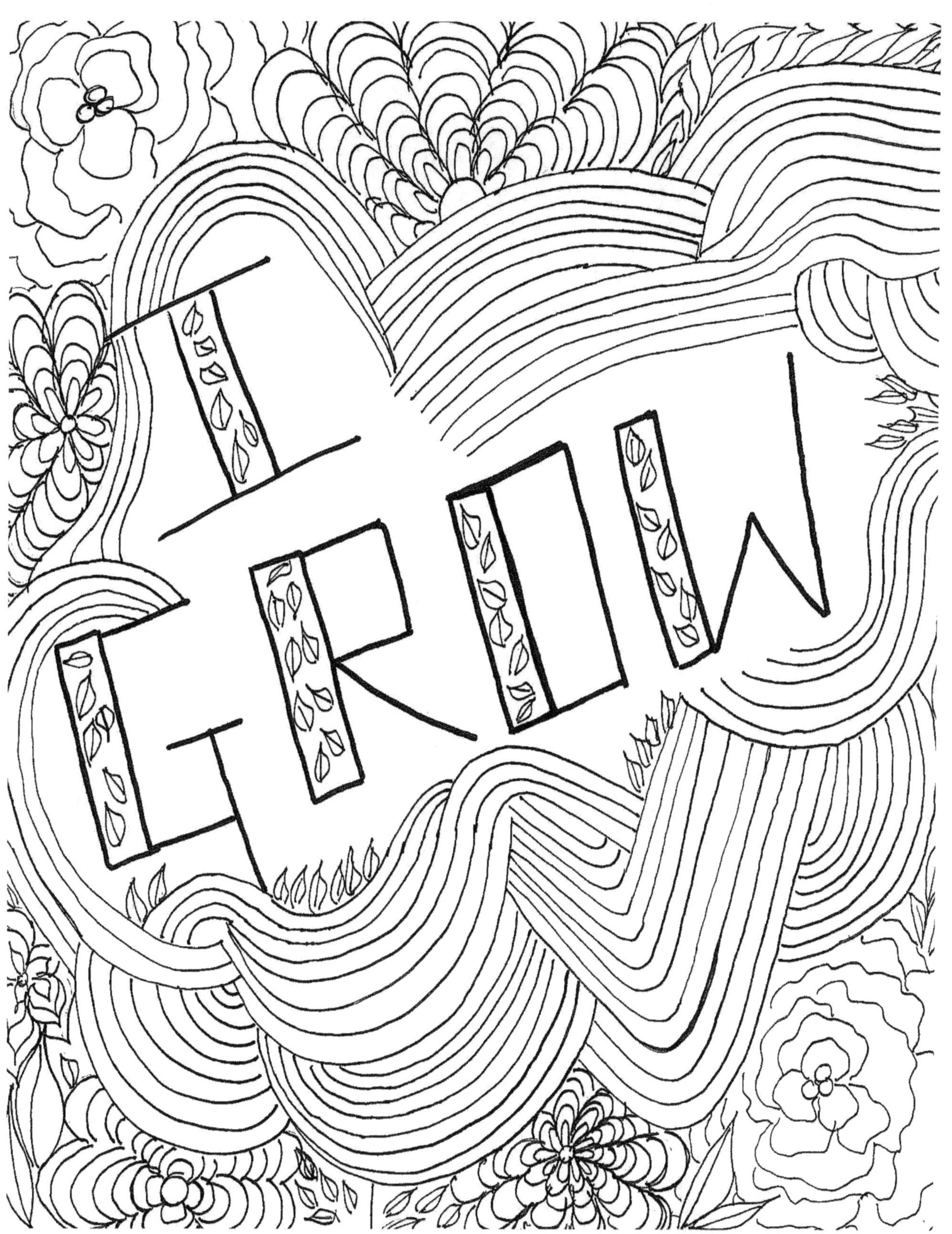
I GROW

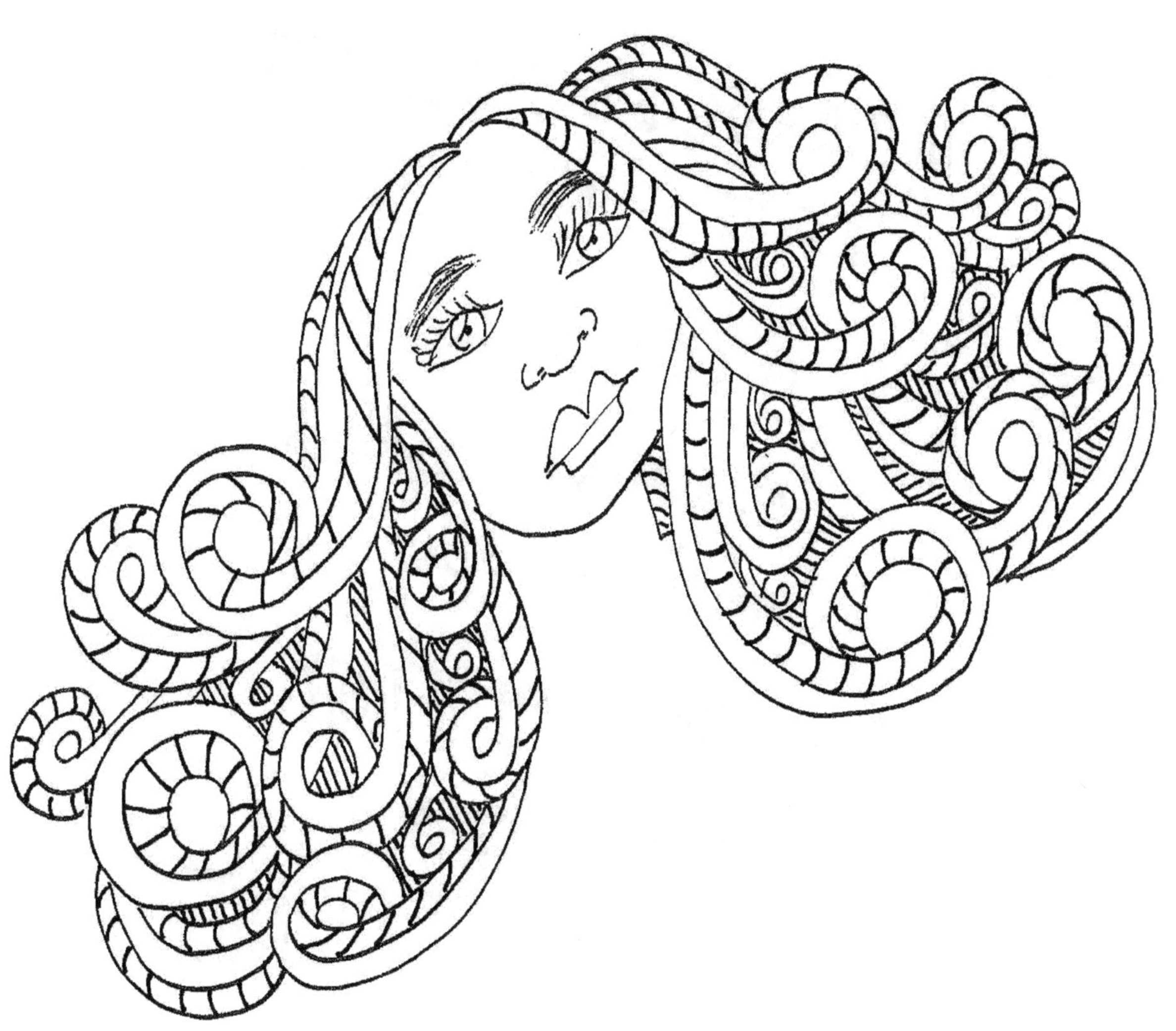

COLOR, EMBELLISH,
TAG AND POST

@clove410

@welovedoodledos

#doodledos

THANK YOU FOR
SHARING &
INSPIRING
OTHERS

RE-MIX

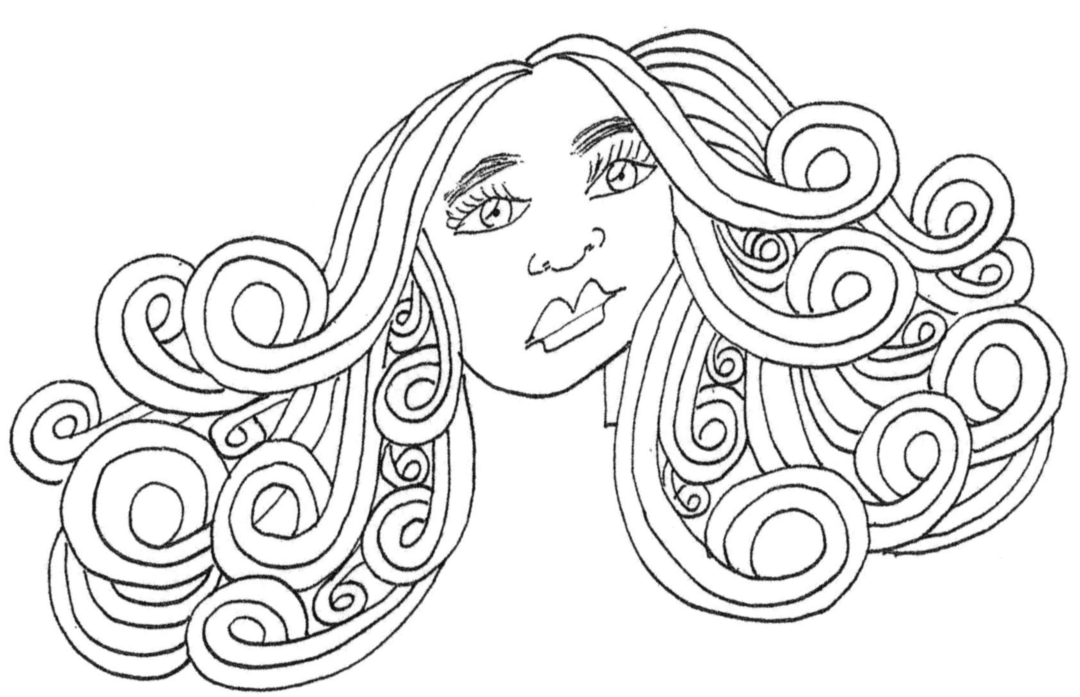

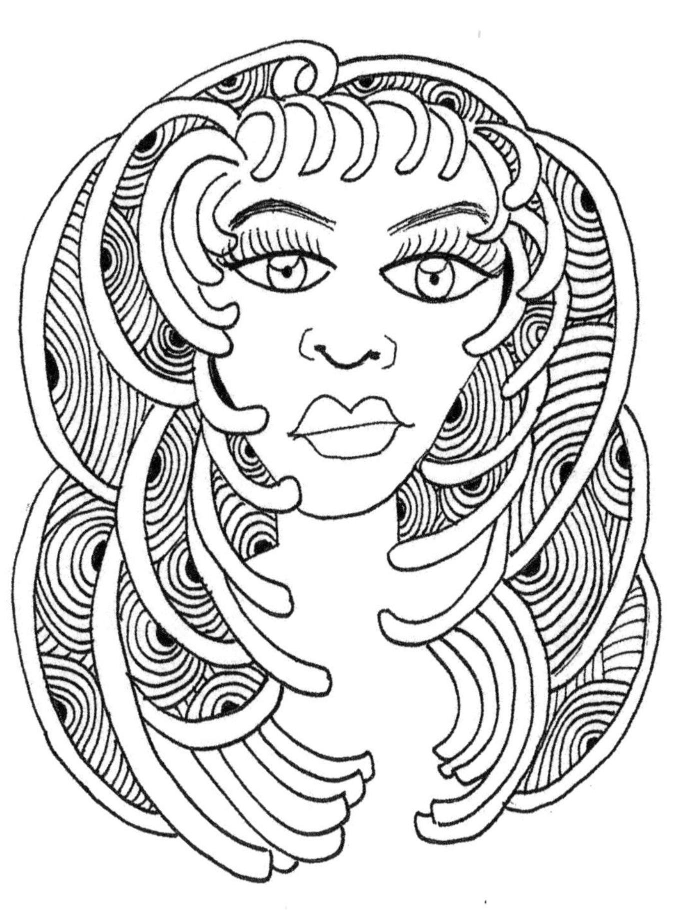

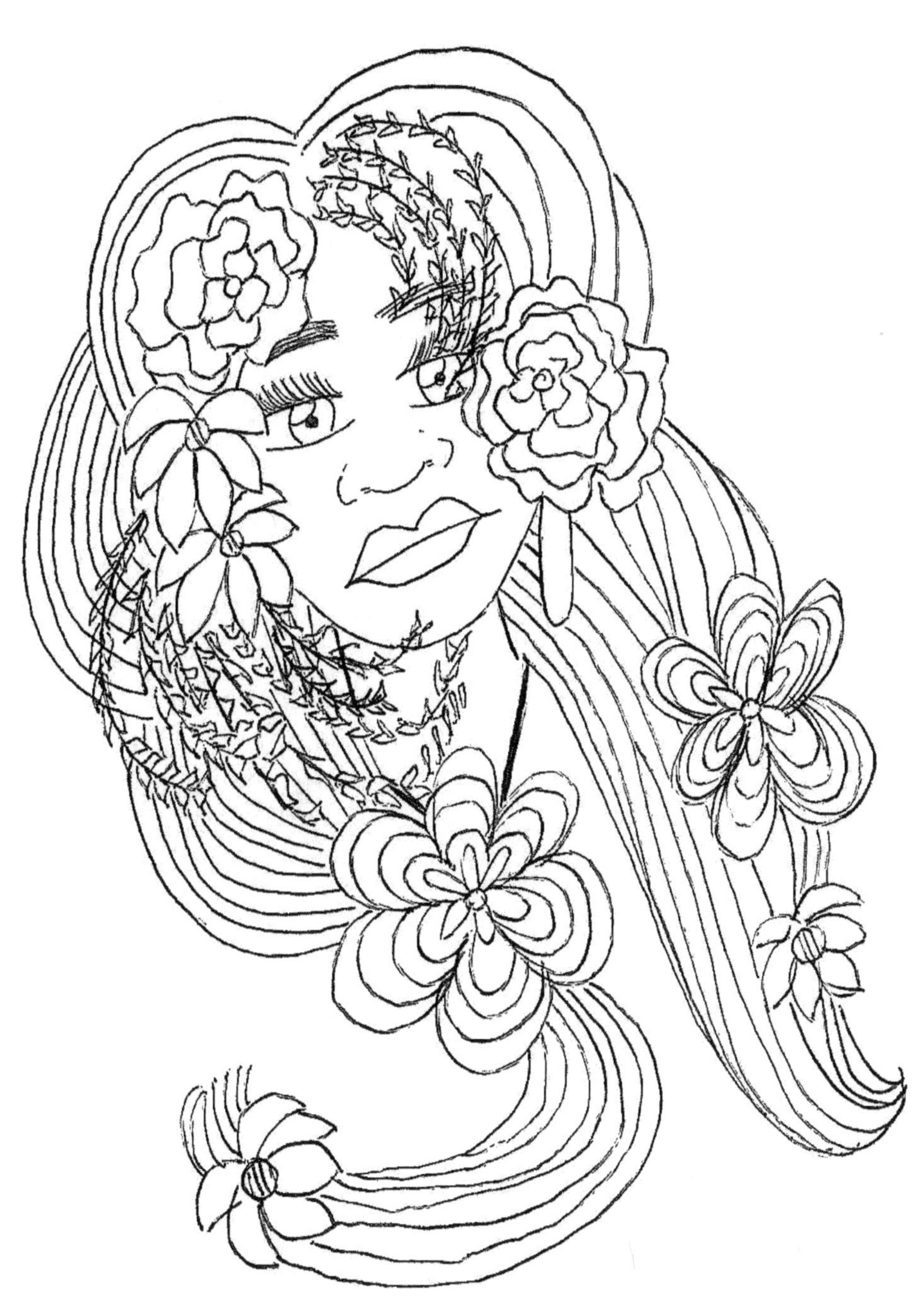

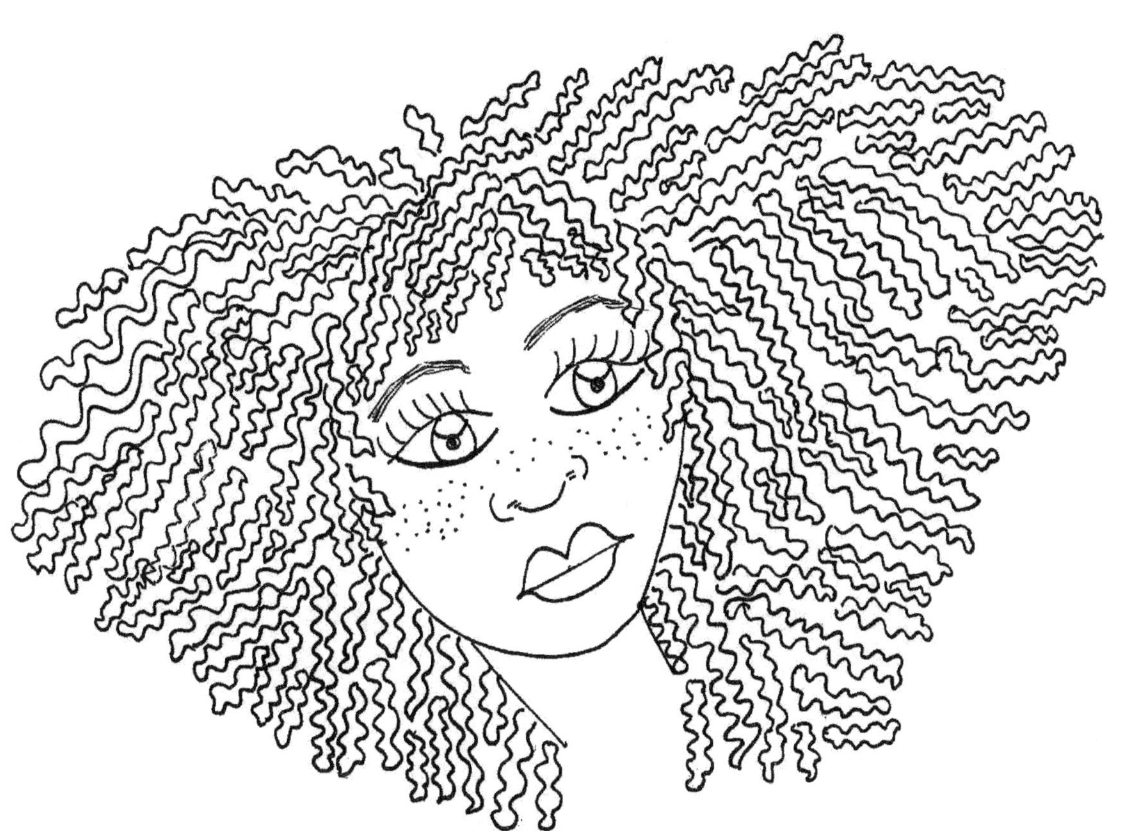

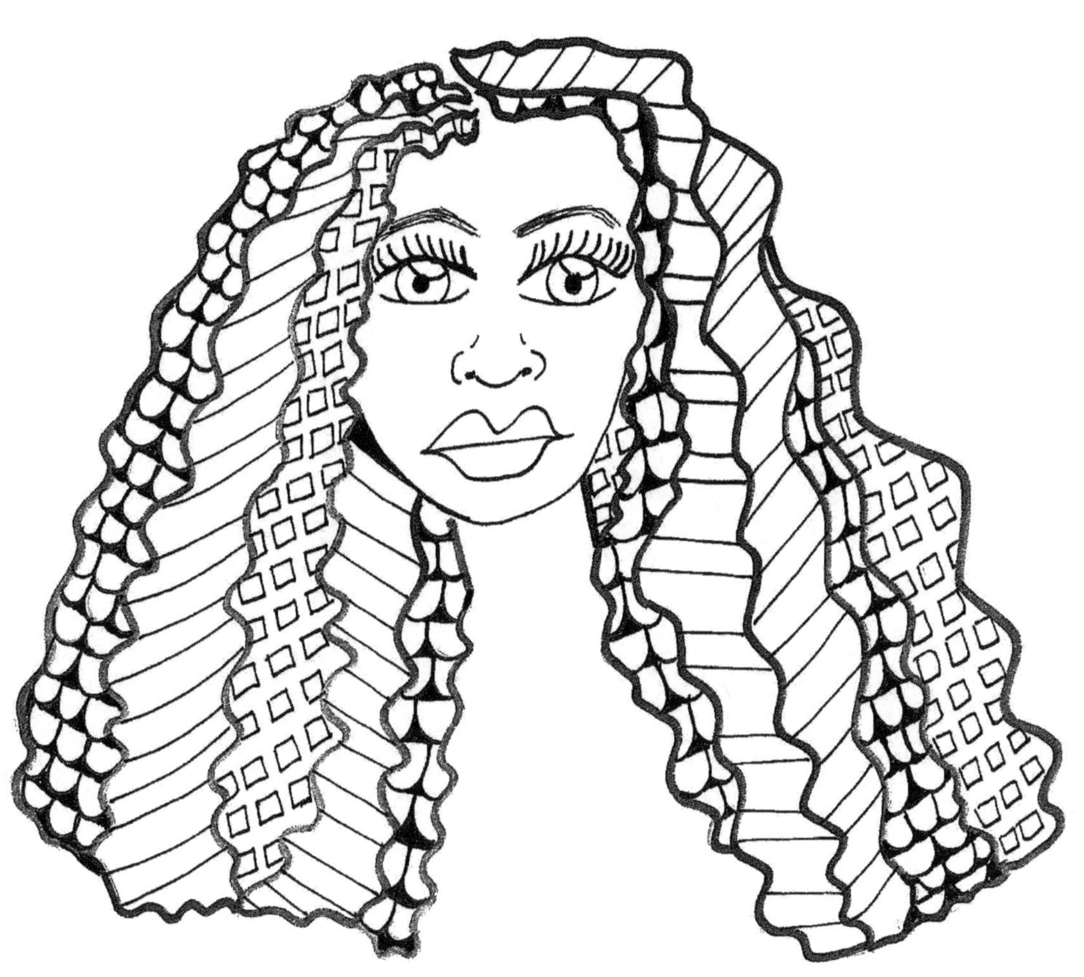

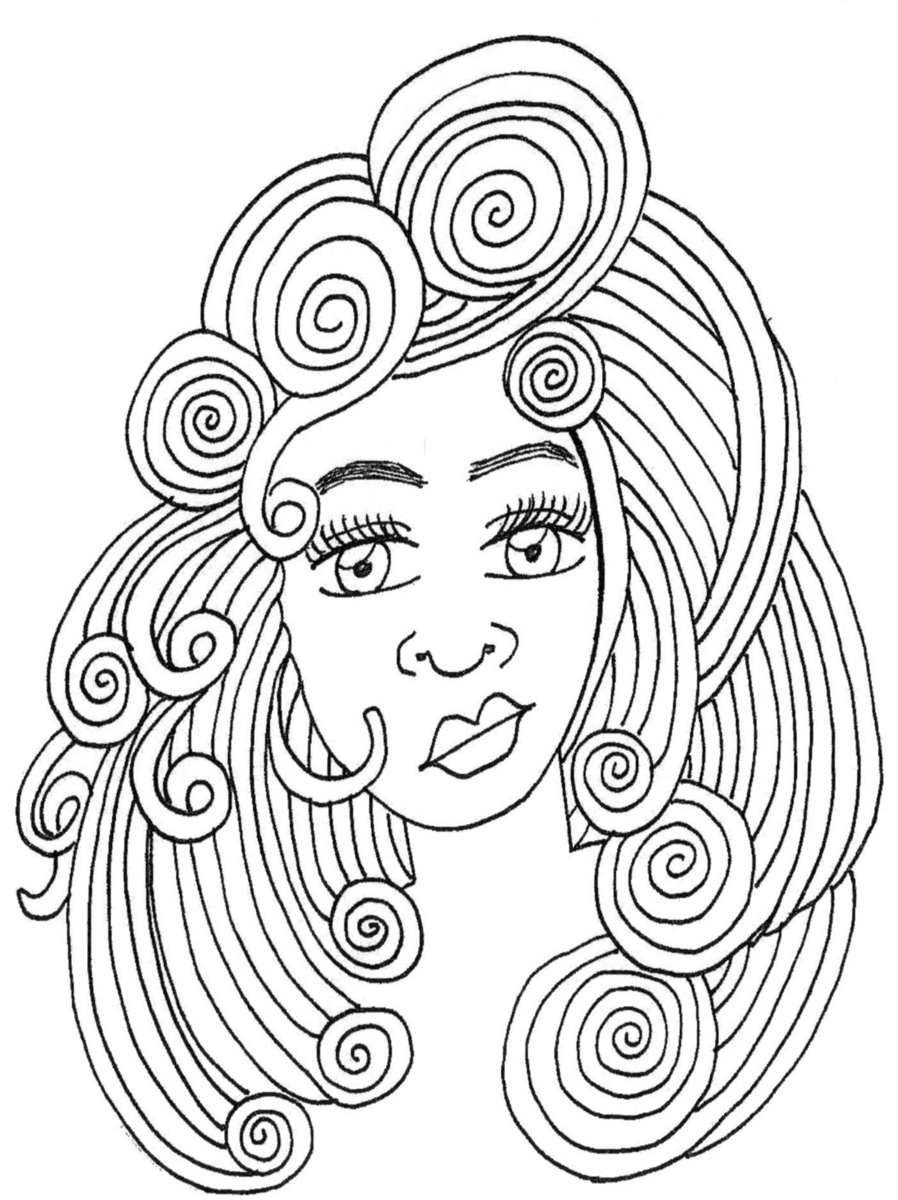

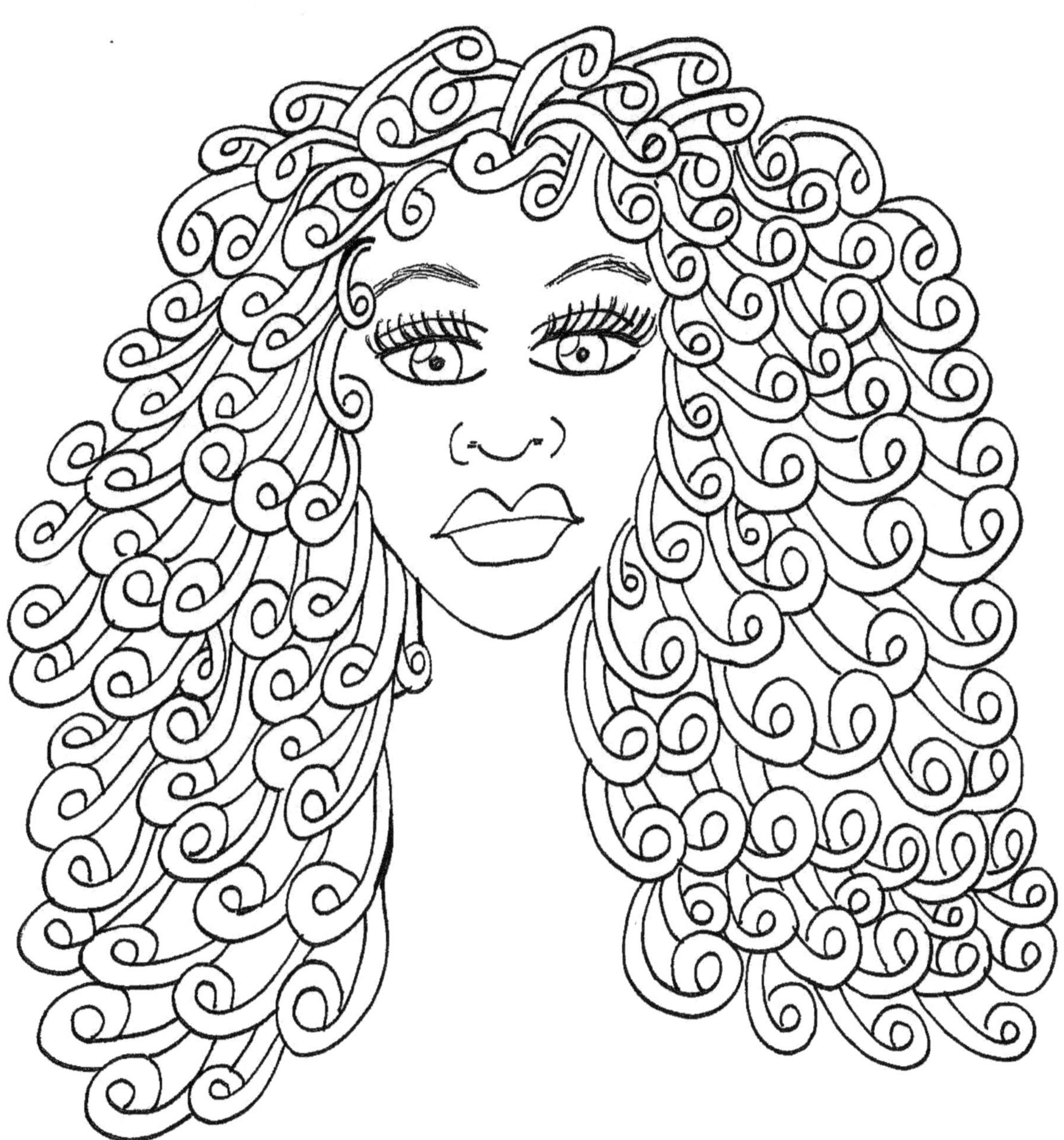

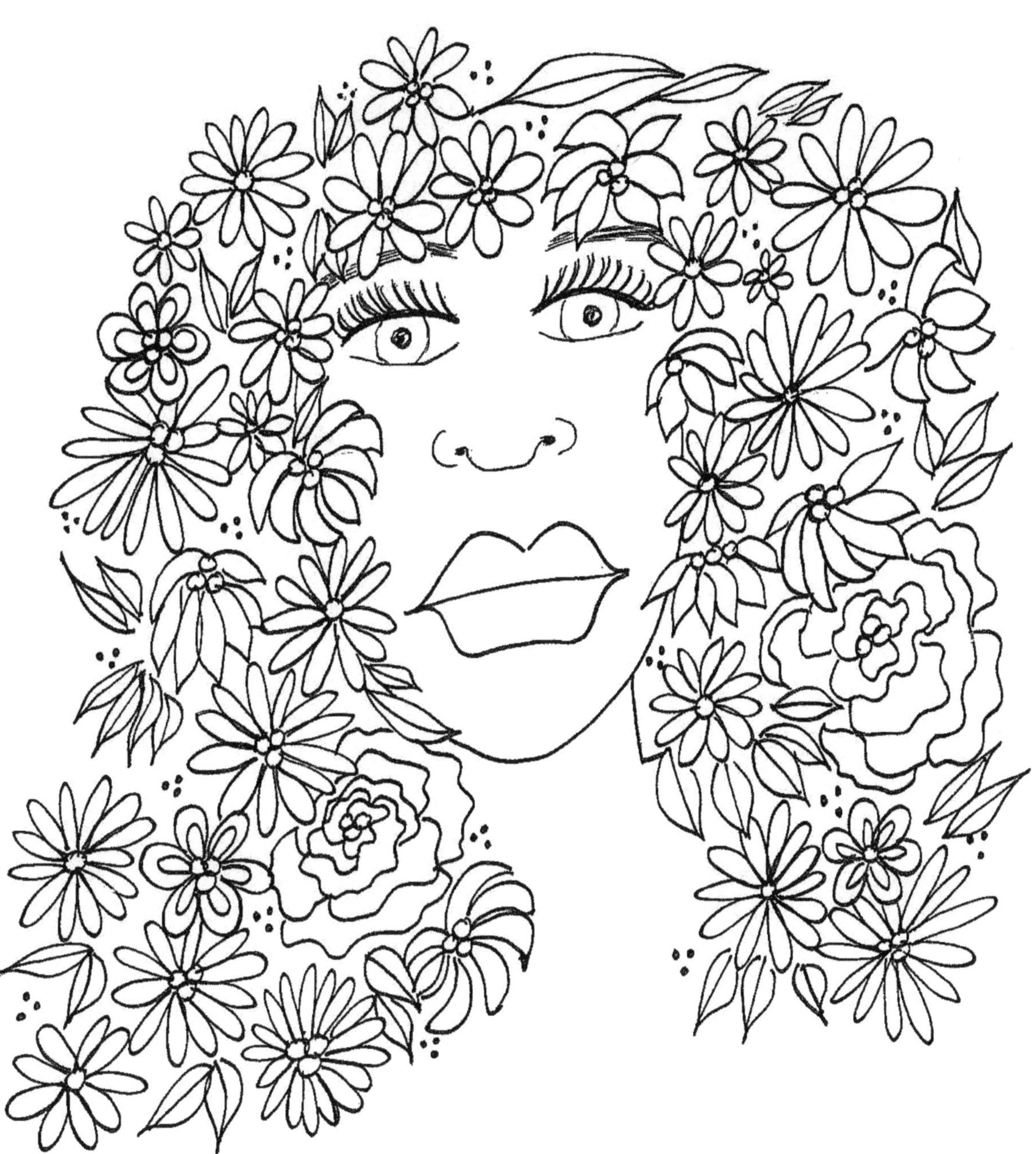

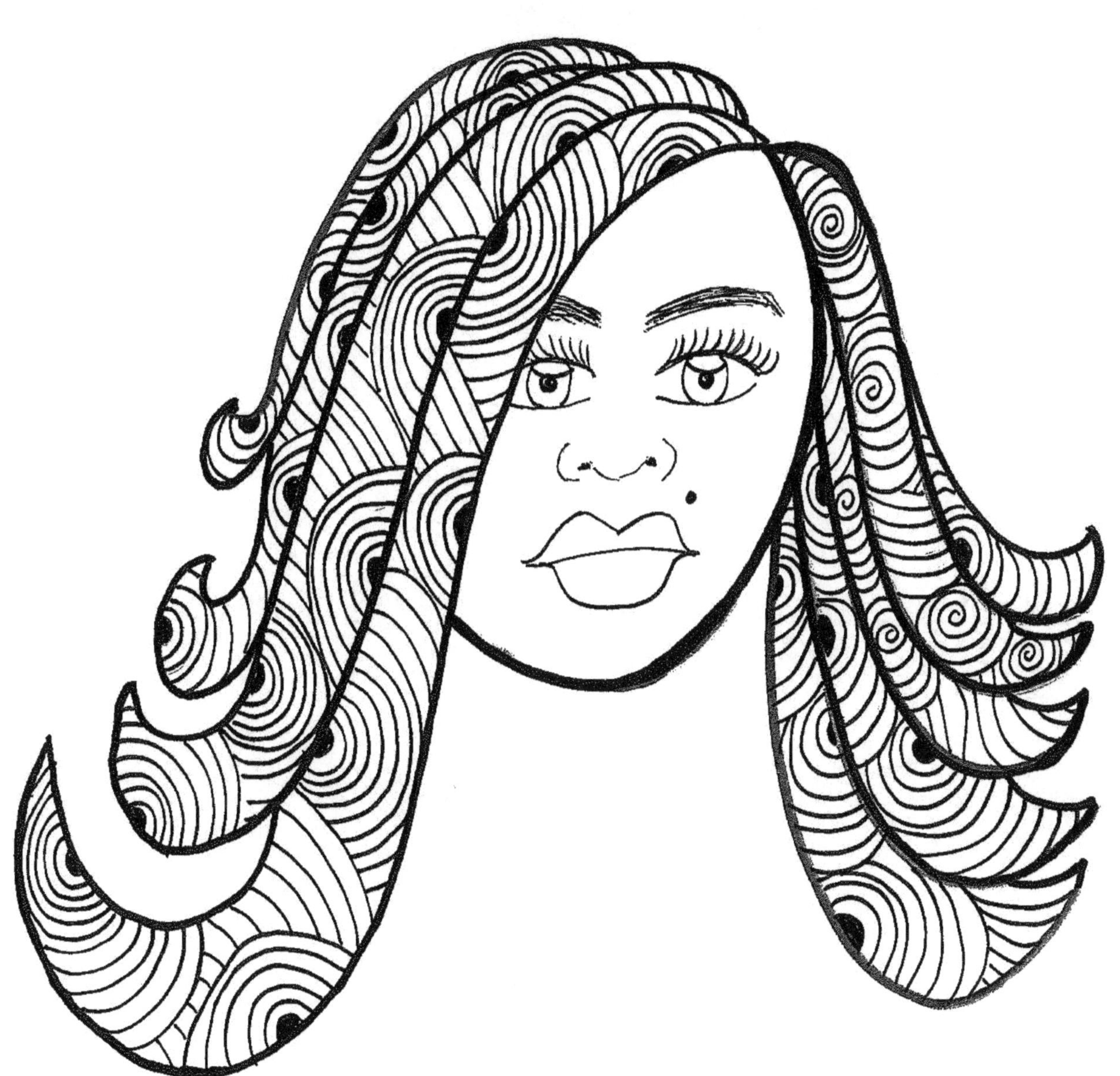

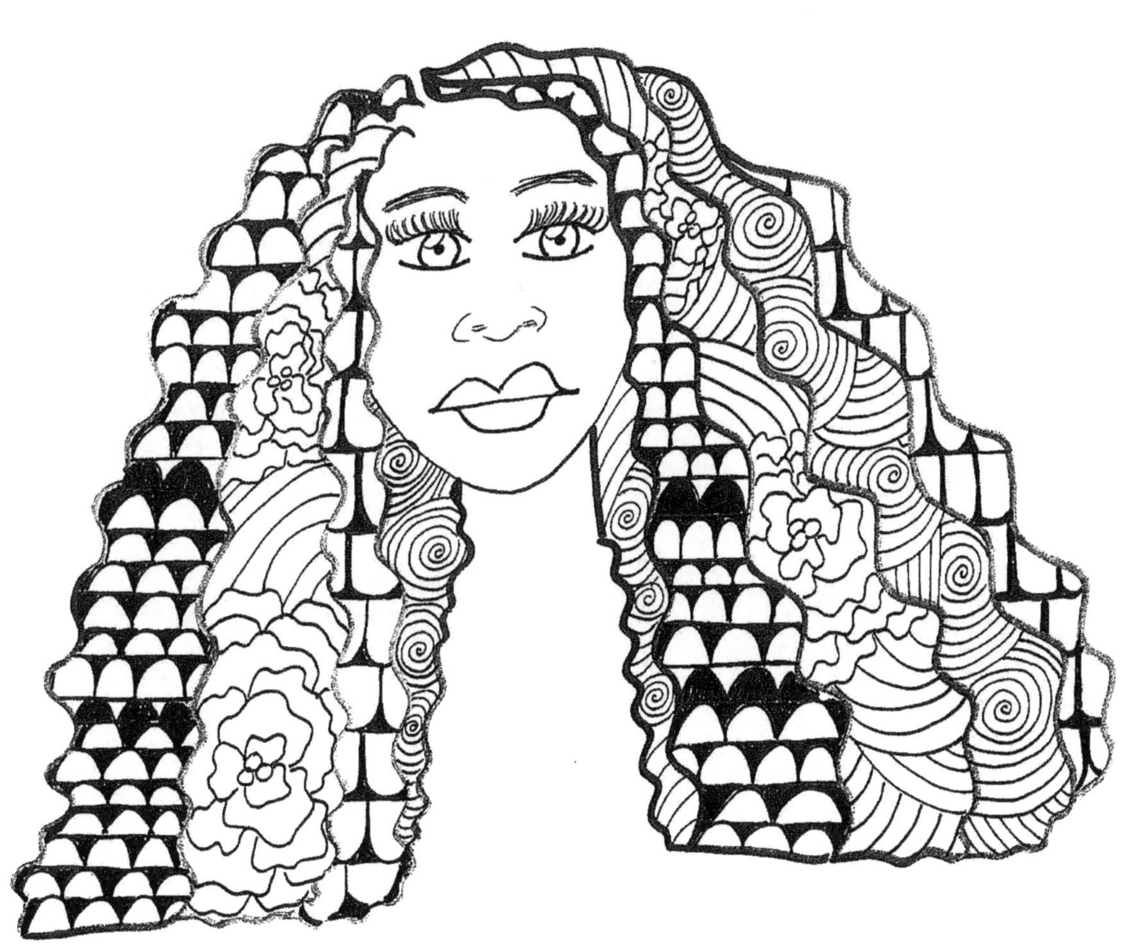

RE-MIX

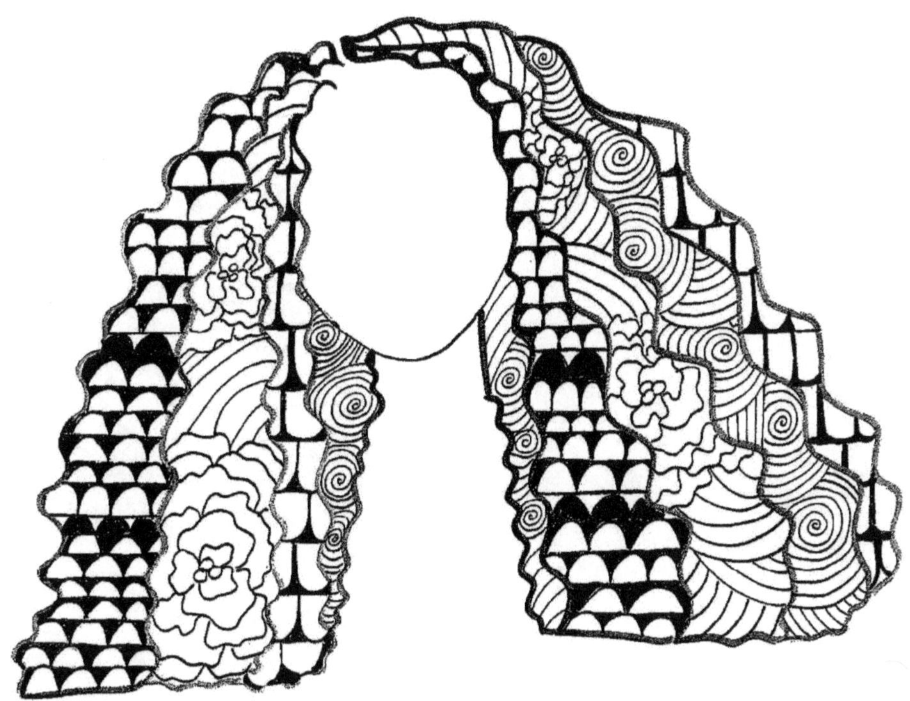

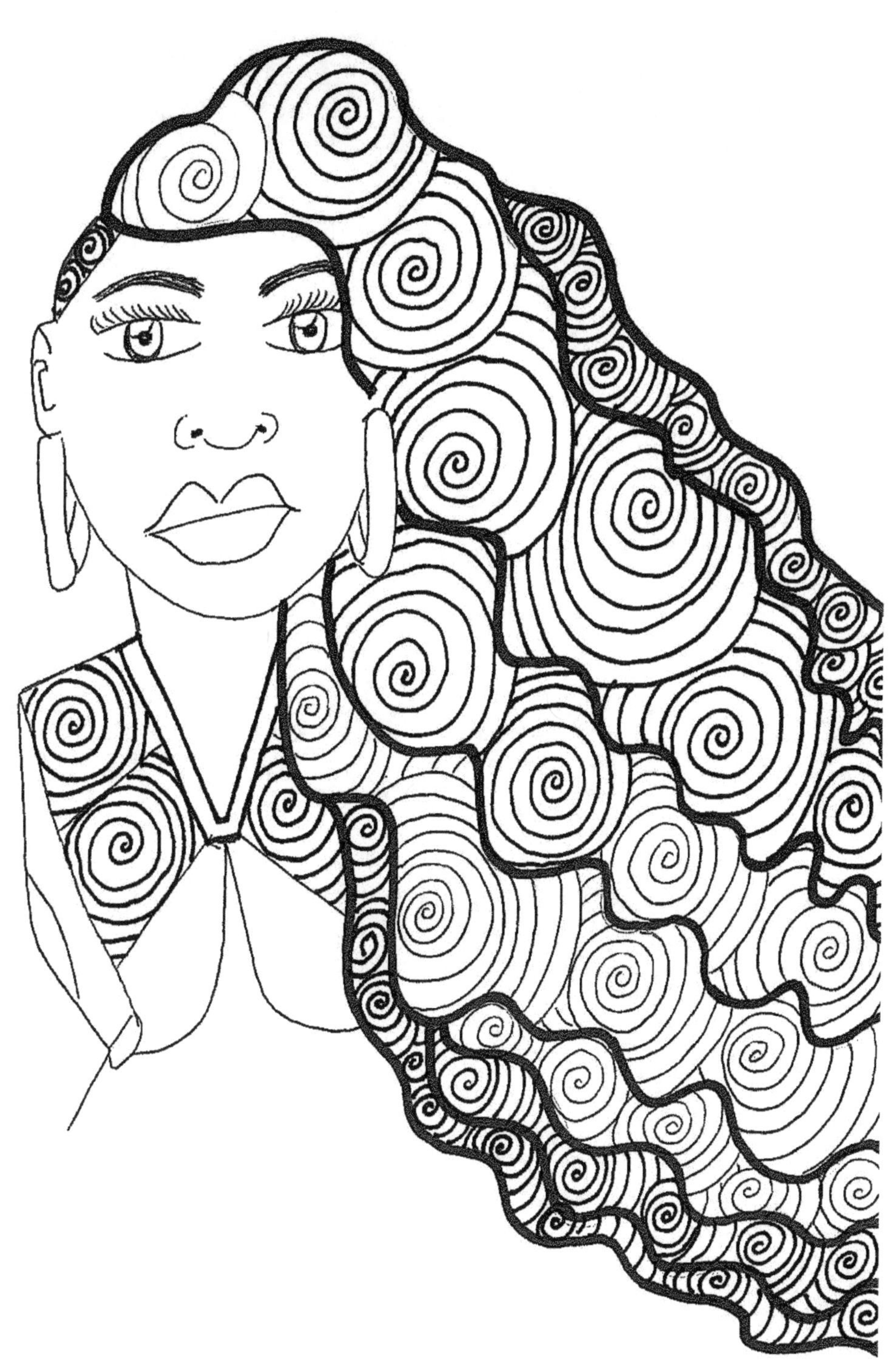

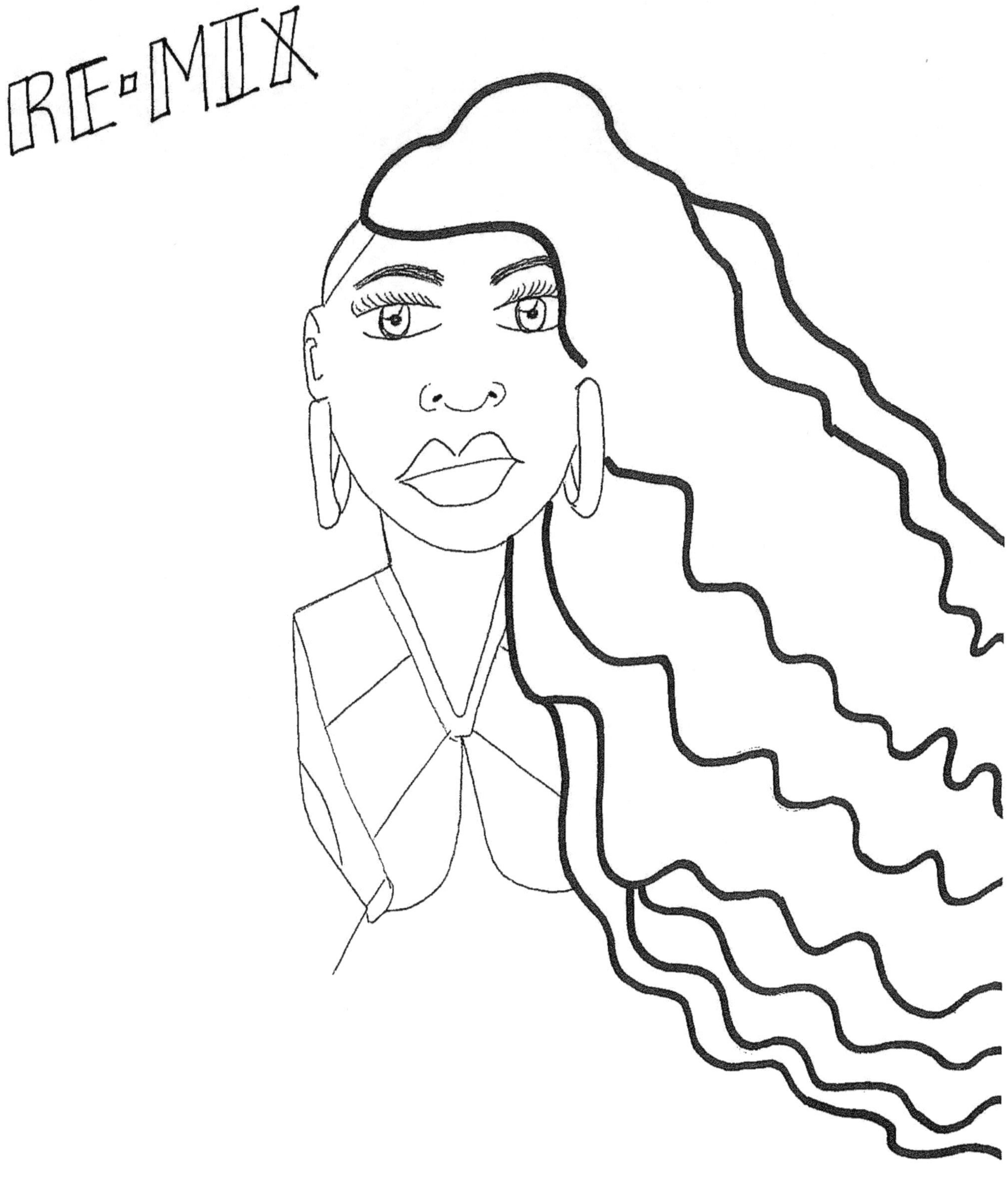

RE-MIX

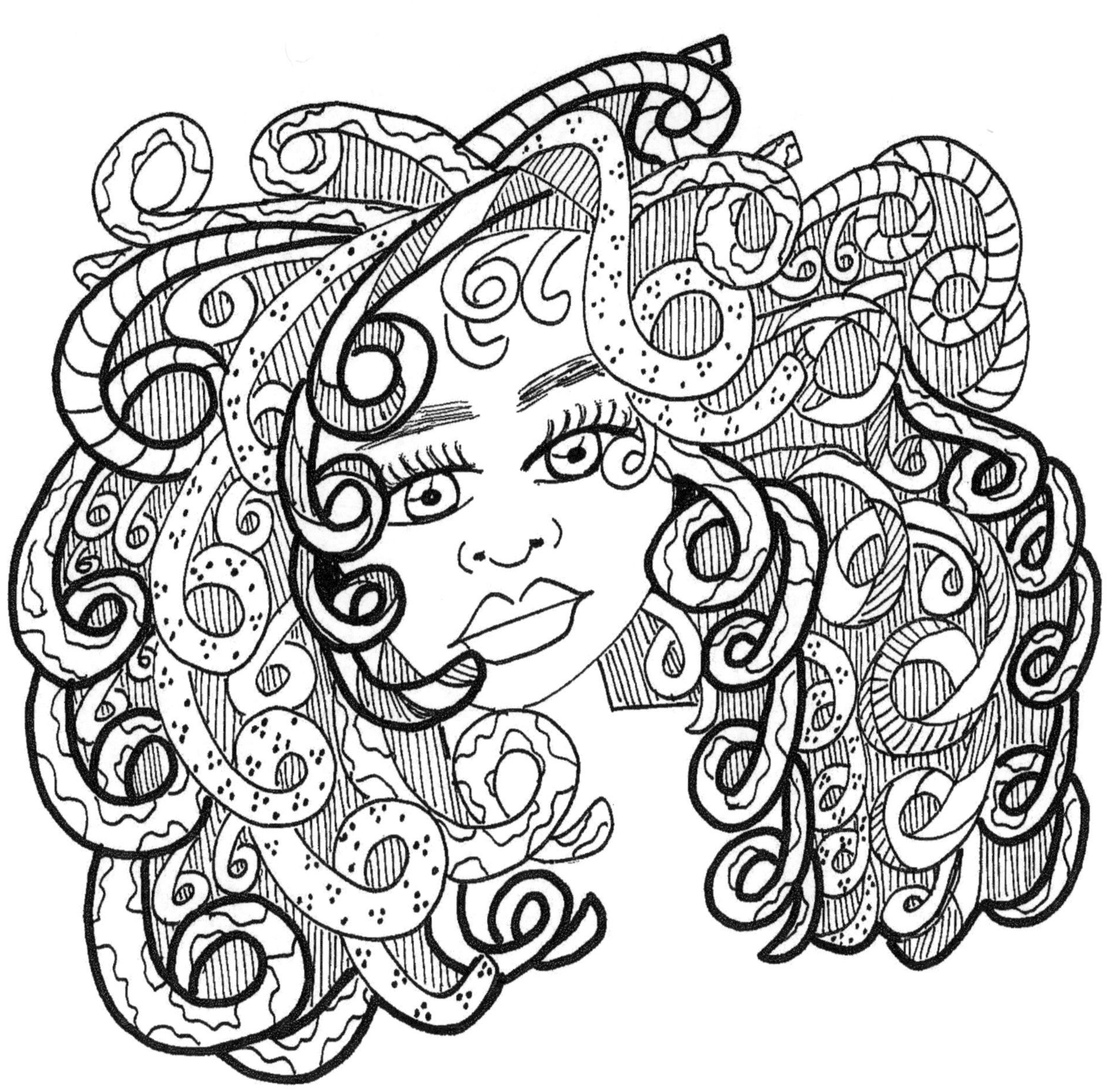

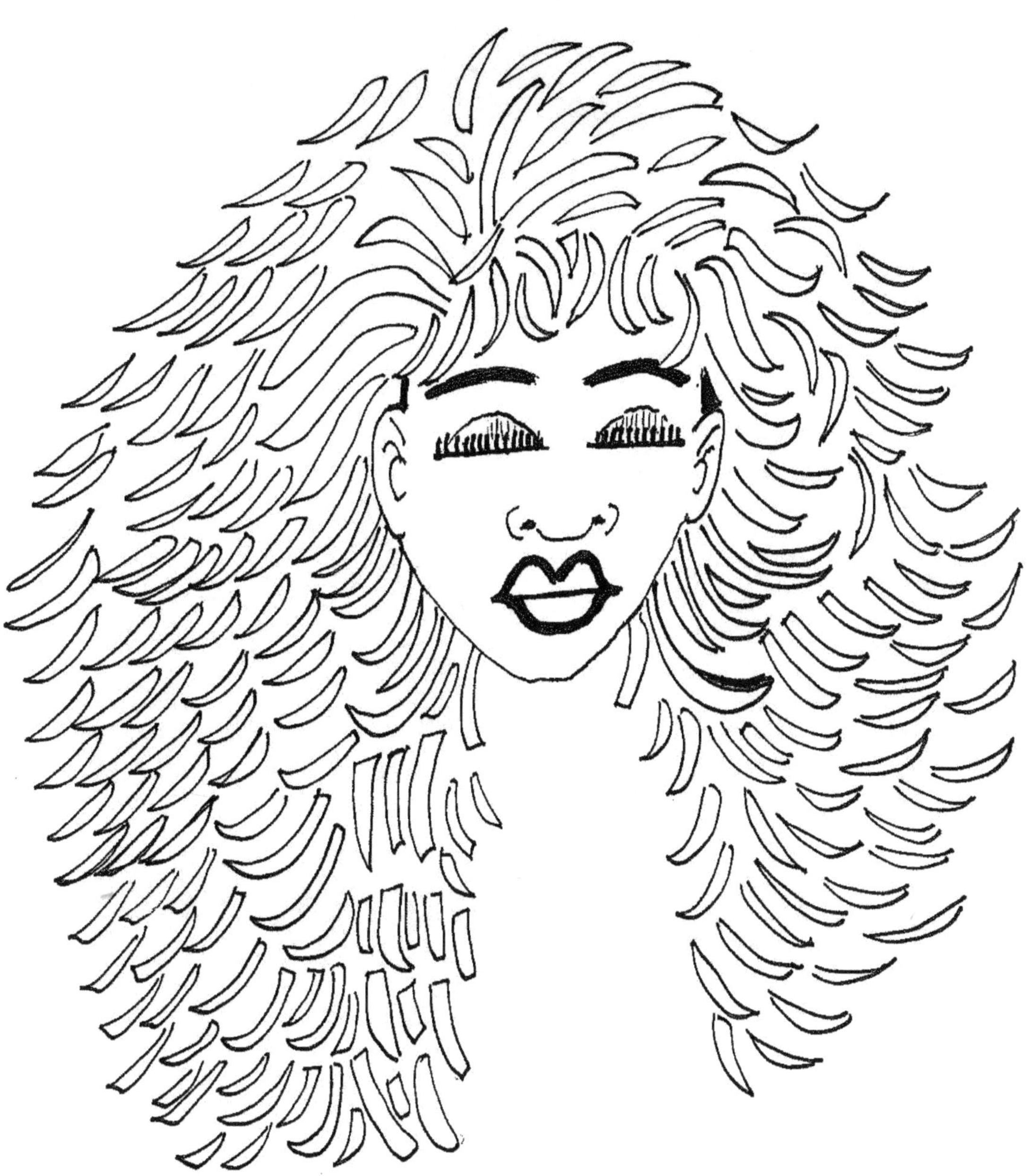

GET CREATIVE!
Techniques:
USE SHAPES YOU KNOW
Tools: PENS PENCILS MARKERS PAINT SHARPIE CRAYONS
Lines:

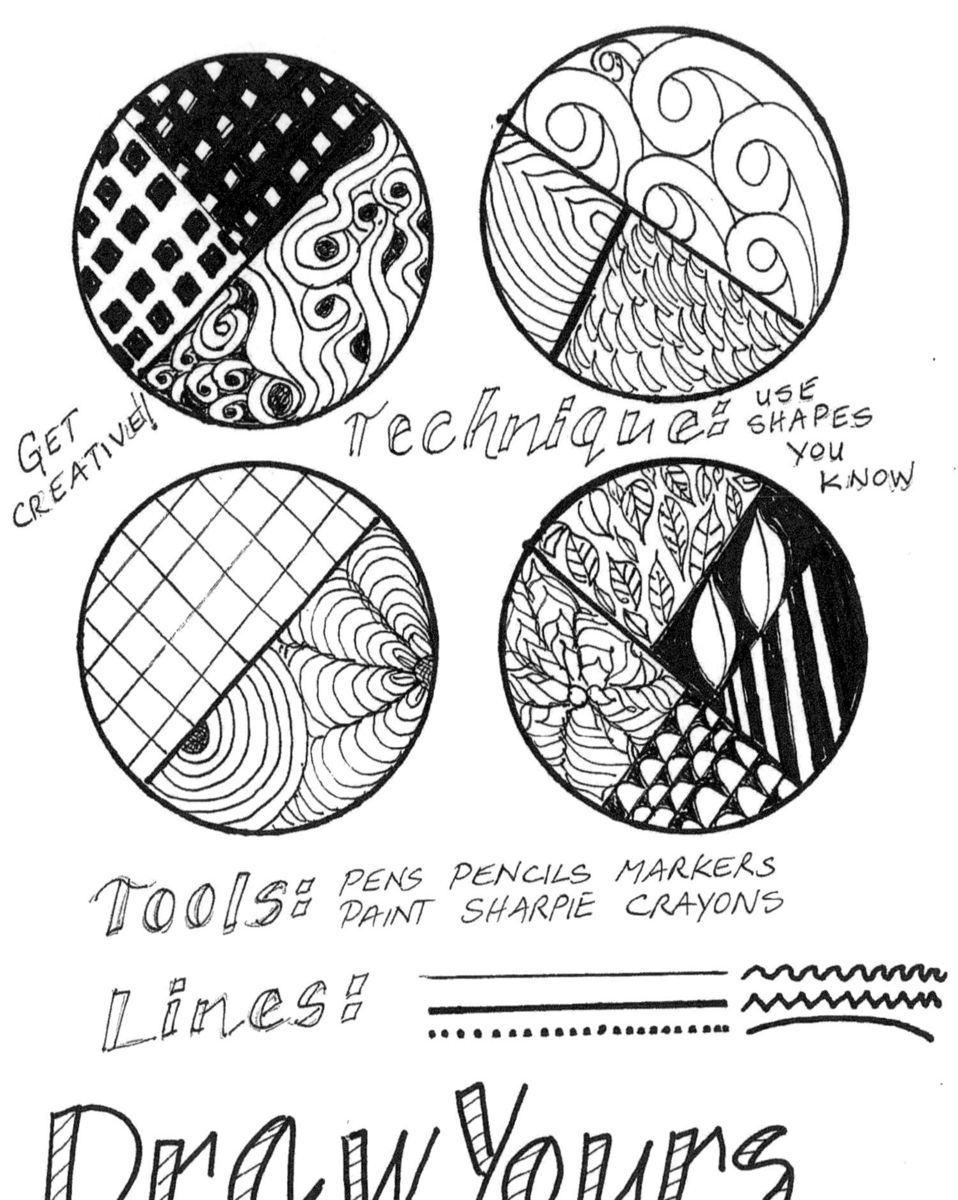

Draw Yours

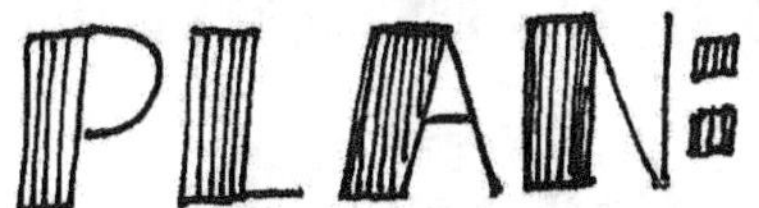

PICK COLORS, ADD LINES/SWIRLS, BOLD OUTLINE, LEAF BORDER, PINK LIP, BROWN EYES...

A = PINK
B = BROWN
OUTLINE = SHARPIE

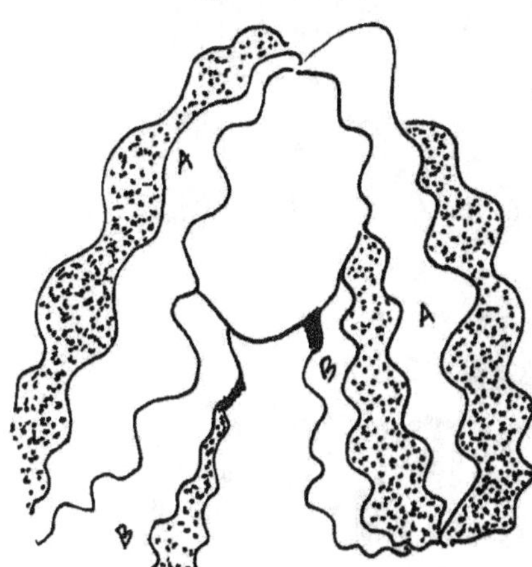

Inspiration!

LOOK AT THE WORLD AROUND YOU—PEOPLE, NATURE - LEAVES, CLOUDS, FLOWERS, FEATHERS, WATER, PATTERNS, NUMBERS, SHAPES, ETC.

STYLES:

CURLS, WAVES, CRIMPS, PLAITS, KNOTS, LOCS, KINKS, BRAIDS, FLIPS, PONYTAIL, BANGS, STRAIGHT—

BIG HAIR DON'T CARE!

FACES:

EYE

LIPS

BROW

NOSE

EAR

Practice

Practice

Practice!

USE NO BLEED MARKERS OR PUT A PIECE OF PAPER UNDER YOUR ART TO PREVENT THE MARKER FROM SEEPING THROUGH THE PAGE.

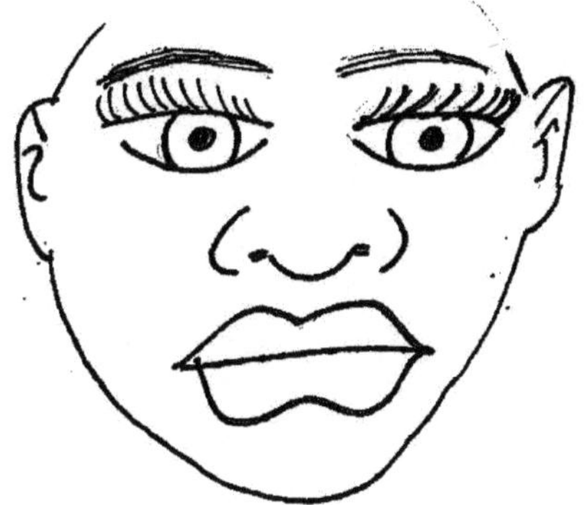

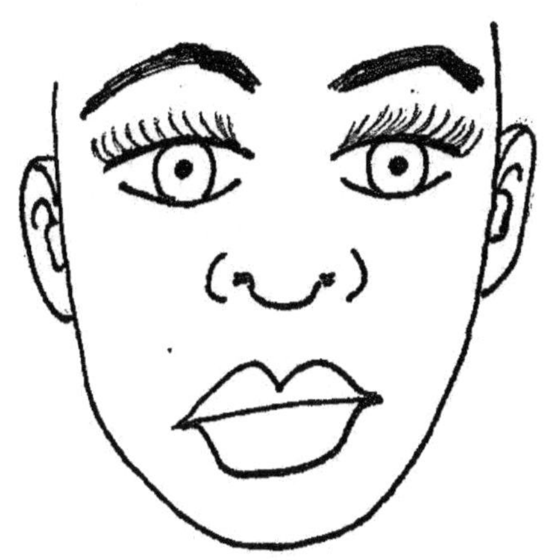

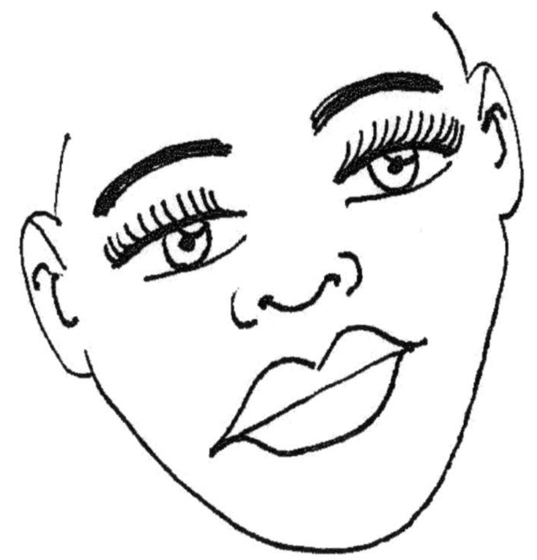

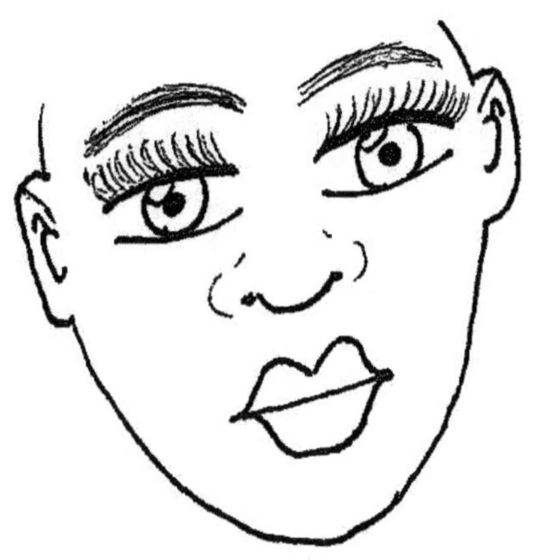

Love you to the moon and back.

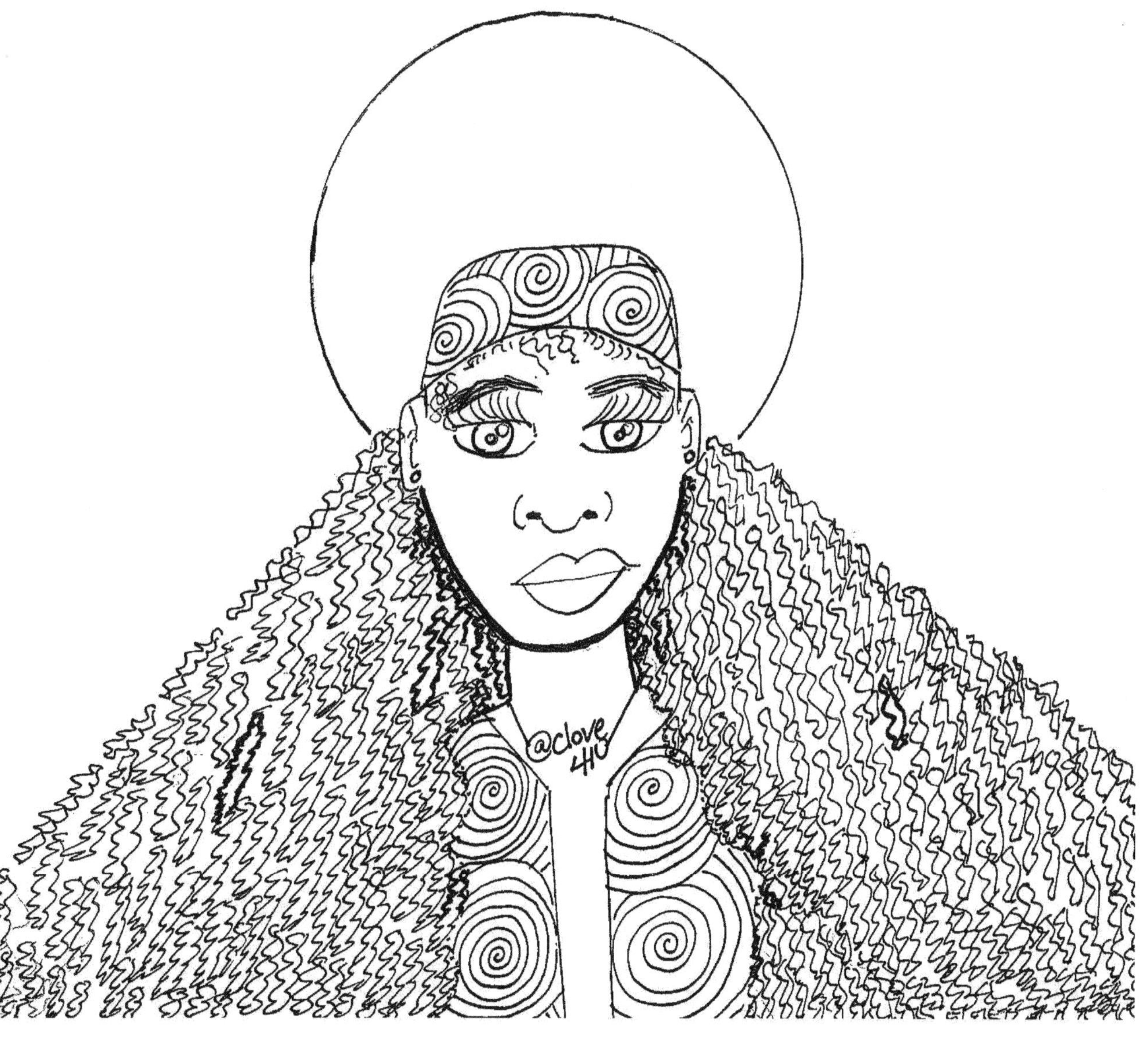

POST YOUR FINISHED PAGES FOR A CHANCE TO WIN JOURNALS, SWAG, BOOKS, ETC.

TAG
@welovedoodledos

#doodledos

REMINDER:
SIGN YOUR ART

www.ingramcontent.com/pod-product-compliance
Lightning Source LLC
La Vergne TN
LVHW081320110826
845149LV00006B/1556
9780998233994